WE'RE STILL COOKING

WE'RE STILL COOKING

REBUILDING MACON

REBUILDING MACON | MACON, GEORGIA | 2016

3864 Lake Street
Macon, Georgia 31204

WE'RE STILL COOKING

First Edition

ISBN-10 0-9753726-1-0
ISBN-13 978-0-9753726-1-6

Book design by Burt&Burt

Printed in Canada

ACKNOWLEDGMENTS

Much like the satisfying sight of Mrs. Vicey Burney singing and clapping with youth volunteers on her front yard, motivating them as they scraped and painted her home—many hands offered the same, sweet support to roll out the second course to Rebuilding Macon's cookbook, *Let's Get Cooking*.

After all, six years later "we're still cooking."

We are grateful to our Board of Directors for allowing us to, once again, pursue this project and for backing us along the way.

We are also very grateful to the owners and chefs of each restaurant represented in this cookbook for their willingness to share a little bit of their history and their recipes with us.

A big, big thank you to Beau Cabell for his beautifully created photographs that had us drooling throughout the entire production process.

We'd also like to thank Skippy Davis for spending time with these food artists and restauranteurs to create profiles that will intrigue your mind and entice your taste buds.

A very special thank you to Jim and Mary-Frances Burt of Burt&Burt for designing another perfectly crafted cookbook.

Last, but not least, we'd like to thank our countless volunteers who work with us to provide rehabilitation services, free of charge, to elderly and disabled low-income homeowners.

We thank each of you for helping us rebuild Macon, one house at a time.

TRUE GRIS

WE KEEP SOME OF OUR FAVORITE RECIPES IN AN OLD TIN BOX. There is no filing system, alphabetical or otherwise, so they defy all laws of organization. They are folded and stuffed inside, like a tightly wrapped burrito.

Many have been written on index cards, others clipped from the food section of the newspaper. Still others have been peeled from the labels of soup cans and cut from the back of cake boxes.

A few bear my mother's cursive writing, time-honored recipes that have crossed five state lines and fed hungry mouths for three generations.

Other recipes are like family heirlooms, passed down from forefathers and grandmothers. They carry the battle scars of the kitchen—smudges and smears of softened butter, bacon grease and gravy stains.

There are orderly lists of ingredients and specific directions for squash casseroles, oatmeal raisin cookies, cheese apples, broccoli-raisin salads and spiced tea. Although most recipes require precise chemistry, we all know the best cooks rarely need to measure. They work without a net, relying on the virtues of instinct and experience. It's the same way great writers find words without a dictionary, artists can brush their pallets blindfolded, and musicians improvise without sheet music. (Still, exactly how much is a pinch of salt? Guess it depends on the size of your fingers.)

Julia Reed once said: "Cookbooks in the South outsell everything but the Bible." Amen to that. I'm proud to hail from a part of the country where macaroni and cheese is considered a vegetable.

In a world of instant oatmeal and microwave mashed potatoes, cookbooks are the soup bones to give us sustenance and flavor. They are reminders of how we ride the apron strings of all those gracious cooks who have blazed trails of peach preserves and ground cumin.

Their recipes represent our culinary genealogies. They have been tweaked and amended over the years. We claim ownership, even if they were passed down from the dear lady who lives across the street from our third cousin's best friend.

At our house, there are dozens of cookbooks, both bought and borrowed. My family's collection are stacked on the shelves like a reference section at the library. On their pages are recipes from saints who still make scratch biscuits and church ladies who bake casseroles for the sick and shut-ins.

For the past six years, our most treasured cookbook has been *Let's Get Cooking*, published by the folks at Rebuilding Macon in 2010. It has a gold-plated, personal place among our silverware. I wrote the foreword and it features the recipe for my signature dish, "True Gris Stew."

Once again, it is an honor to have been asked to do the foreword to the newest collection of recipes from some of Macon's finest restaurants.

As many of you know, my mother's name is Charlie. She was named after her father, who died before she was born in 1928. Having a male name has put her in some interesting situations over the years. She was assigned to a men's dormitory when she enrolled at the University of Georgia. When she was a stewardess for Delta Airlines in the 1950s, her name would always raise a few eyebrows when the pilot would announce it over the intercom. (There were no male flight attendants back in those days.)

She was a home economics major in college, and taught it in high school for a few years after she graduated. So, mama does know how to cook.

I could have chosen several of her recipes to share with you, but her artichoke salad has always been a showstopper. I hope you enjoy it. And thank you for supporting Rebuilding Macon and the blessing they are to our community.

— Ed Grisamore

MAMA CHARLIE'S ARTICHOKE SALAD

1 box chicken Rice-a-Roni cooked and cooled.
1 jar marinated artichokes, with marinade.
1/3 cup Duke's mayonnaise
1/4 teaspoon curry
Small bunch of well-chopped green onions
Small jar stuffed green olives, chopped

Mix all together and serve at room temperature

Ed Grisamore is a journalism, storytelling, and creative writing instructor at Stratford Academy in Macon as well as a columnist for The Telegraph. *He is the author of nine books and recipient of the 2010 Will Rogers Humanitarian Award, presented by the National Society of Newspaper Columnists.*

NOW,

LET'S GET COOKING

Lacresia Sacre and Gloria Cla

1842 INN

MOST COUPLES WHO CHOOSE TO MARRY AT THE 1842 INN SELECT THE INN'S FRONT STEPS for the wedding ceremony, often with a harpist providing the music.

"But others may choose to have the wedding in the backyard garden, sometimes followed by a wedding breakfast," said E J Nobles, manager of guest services for the Inn. "Often we have the wedding outside and the reception indoors."

A wedding and reception including some 50 to 75 guests is just a part of the lovely Inn's busy schedule. On Sundays through Thursdays, it is common to have corporate business travelers staying overnight. "Women's organizations, such as the Colonial Dames, have held meetings at the Inn and stayed overnight as well," Mr. Nobles said, and a full complimentary breakfast is served daily.

With 19 rooms, the Inn can accommodate many guests, and as might be expected, its kitchen can be a busy place. Lacresia Sacre is director of food and catering and has worked at the Inn for nine years. Originally from Utah, she cooks for the guests on Mondays and Fridays, shops for food and takes care of catering events.

"I love what I do," Ms. Sacre said. "We want people to feel at home when they come here."

Gloria Clark has been the Inn's cook for 20 years. Smiling, she said, "Cooking and catering feels good to me. It never feels like work."

"We're known as a small boutique inn," Mr. Nobles said, "but a lot of our services are amenities that you'd find in a larger property. We get a lot of people coming here from Atlanta, Columbus and Savannah, but we have many guests from out-of-state and international guests as well."

Guests are always welcome to stay for one night, but weekend stays are probably the most popular, Mr. Nobles said. "And we get a lot of corporate business travelers Sundays through Thursdays. People like to stay at an inn."

What draws many people to Macon is the opportunity to view the city's beautiful historic homes. Mr. Nobles calls that "the antebellum experience." Macon's music heritage—Otis Redding, James Brown, the Allman Brothers, H&H Restaurant, and others—is a major enticement that brings visitors to Macon and to the Inn.

The 1842 Inn, located on historic College Street, opened as a bed and breakfast in the early 1980s. Through the years its reputation as both an elegant and delightful place to stay has spread throughout Georgia and beyond. Its owners are Ed and Beverly Knight Olson.

FRENCH TOAST

INGREDIENTS

2 slices of thick French bread
1 egg
1/4 cup of fresh orange juice
Butter
Cream cheese
Peach preserve
Whipped cream
Powdered sugar

PREPARATION

Mix some cream cheese and peach preserve together and spread between the two slices of bread.

Soak the French bread in the egg and orange juice that has been mixed together.

Heat butter in a skillet and brown each side of the French bread.

Spread more peach preserves on top and add fresh whipped cream.

Sprinkle entire plate with powdered sugar and garnish with a fresh mint sprig.

Serves 1

ENGLISH SCONES

INGREDIENTS

8 cups biscuit mix
1/2 cup crushed pecans
1/2 cup sugar
1 1/2 cup currants
5 eggs
1 cup heavy whipping cream
Flour for dusting

PREPARATION

Preheat oven to 350 degrees.

Mix all the ingredients in a large bowl until mixture forms into a ball.

Spread some flour onto the rolling surface and roll out the dough to about half-inch thick.

Cut out the scones with a biscuit cutter.

Bake scones on a lightly greased baking sheet for 15 to 20 minutes or until brown.

Yeilds 35

MINT JULEP

INGREDIENTS

Handful of fresh mint

1 ounce Southern Comfort
or bourbon of choice

1/2 ounce Amber Bacardi Rum

2 drops Angostura
aromatic bitters

Lemon slice for garnish

Sugar

PREPARATION

Boil mint until water turns green. Strain the mint water into a glass pitcher.

Add one cup of sugar for each quart of water while hot to create a mint syrup. *Mint syrup can be kept refrigerated for three days.*

Fill a silver, mint julep cup with ice and add one ounce of bourbon and a half-ounce of rum.

Stir in your mint syrup until cup is filled.

Add two drops of bitters and garnish with lemon and fresh mint.

Serves 1

AUBRI LANE'S

WHEN WALKING UP TO AUBRI LANE'S, one can see from the sign and building that the restaurant is a bit different from the many bars and pubs that line the streets of Milledgeville. Inside, a long staircase curves along the left side of the restaurant and leads to the second floor offering a 22 person private dining room and 40 capacity mezzanine seating. The open concept is airy and elegant but touches of wood and brick offer a rustic feel. The building has some unique features that are inherent to its history.

Jason Medders was watching a show featuring Paula Dean's restaurant one night and got to thinking about what he might name his restaurant. He knew the place would offer Southern cuisine and so he asked his wife, "What about Aubri Lane's?" When she didn't reject the name, he knew that was going to be it. The name offers that Southern sounding charm and comes from his two kids, Aubri and Lane, showcasing the importance of family.

Something else that's important to Jason is offering a seasonal menu and relying on local farmers markets for products used in popular dishes. All items are crafted from scratch by his culinary team including sauces and dressings. They change the menu about 5 to 6 times a year depending on what produce is in season.

First occupied in 1884 during a time where only 6,000 residents called Milledgeville home, Aubri Lane's was a bank known as the Milledgeville Banking Company. Jason will tell you that a great deal of work went into not just transitioning the building into a restaurant, but in preserving the history of the building. Listed on the National Registry of Historic Places, the hammered tin ceiling and the bank's original vault were kept original and are well-maintained. The vault sits to the right of the bar area with its large door open so that diners can view a unique piece of history. However, there is no longer cash stored in the vault but something many might consider just as lavish—wine. Now a wine cellar, the vault is home to a table or two offering patrons a more secluded spot to talk and dine by candlelight.

If you're looking for an affordable, quality meal check out Aubri Lane's in Milledgeville and be sure to ask your waiter about wine pairings from the vault.

ason Medders

MARINATED RACK OF LAMB

INGREDIENTS

Half rack of double
cut as lamb lollipops

4 whole garlic cloves

1 cup extra virgin olive oil

1/4 cup fresh thyme, chopped

1/4 cup fresh Rosemary, chopped

1 tablespoon capers

1 teaspoon cracked red pepper

1/3 cup brown sugar

1/2 lemon, juiced and zested

Salt and pepper to taste

PREPARATION

Add all ingredients into a large mixing bowl and let the lamb rest inside the marinade for 30 minutes.

Portion out rack evenly and put into separate vacuum seal bags.

Refrigerate up to 72 hours before grilling to medium temperature.

Serves 1

PECAN CRUSTED NORTH CAROLINA TROUT

Serves 1

INGREDIENTS

8-10 ounces rainbow trout

2-3 cups pecan flour

2 tablespoons oil

1 tablespoon butter

1/2 lemon, *squeezed*

PREPARATION

If unable to buy pecan flour, run 1 cup pecans through food processor and combine with 2 cups flour.

Coat fish with pecan flour. Heat 2 tablespoons of oil in a sauté pan and sauté the fish until golden brown.

Remove fish from pan. In the same pan, scrape bits from pan, add a tablespoon of butter, a squeeze of fresh lemon juice, and stir until reduced and drizzle over fish.

Served best with a side of collard greens and smoked cheddar grits.

SESAME SEARED AHI TUNA

INGREDIENTS

4 ounces ahi tuna filet
1/4 cup olive oil
Sesame seeds
Crispy wonton chips
1 cup Asian slaw
2 tablespoons teriyaki sauce
2 tablespoons wasabi aioli or mayo

PREPARATION

Preheat skillet with the olive oil.

Pat tuna with sesame seeds and sear tuna for 30 seconds on each side. Slice tuna into thin slices.

Arrange crispy wontons on plate. Top each wonton with a spoonful of Asian slaw, a slice of tuna, a drizzle of wasabi aioli and a drizzle of teriyaki reduction.

Serves 1 to 2

Julio Rosa

THE BACK BURNER

THE BACK BURNER, WELL-KNOWN TO MACON DINERS FOR MANY YEARS, continues to thrive since coming under new ownership in early 2015.

Chef Julio Rosas and his wife, Karen, purchased the restaurant from their friend and chef, Christian Losito, who, after some 18 to 20 years in the kitchen, was considering at least a partial retirement. The two chefs had worked together previously, and the transition of ownership was easy and quick.

"Doors just started to open," Chef Rosas said. "Every door we knocked on just opened, like it was meant to be."

"Everything was easy," Karen added.

After purchasing the popular restaurant, the couple closed it down for just over one week while they accomplished some additional seating, a few changes to the menu, and a fresh appearance throughout the building.

"We did make changes from the previous menu, but we kept a lot of dishes, such as the Sea Bass and others that we knew people loved," Chef Rosas said. "The menu hasn't changed again since we opened."

Karen, who is a social worker and program manager for the juvenile courts, had never been in the restaurant business before. She keeps the restaurant's books up to date, but added with a grin, "I would not be a good server, but when things get busy, I can bus tables like the best of them."

The couple said they feel fortunate that many of The Back Burner's longtime customers have remained loyal to the restaurant and dine there frequently.

"We've been very fortunate to have kept a lot of regulars and others who knew Chef Julio from other restaurants," Karen said.

Chef Rosas has been in the restaurant business for 23 years, having started at the MidTown Grill and later as executive chef for 10 years at Tic Toc Room in downtown Macon where, he said, "Cesare Mammarella gave me so much freedom and let me be creative."

While at the helm of The Back Burner, Chef Rosas entered the Girl Scout Cookie Competition—creating a dessert from a single Girl Scout cookie—and won first place two years in a row.

Chef Rosas is not the only member of his family to be successful in the restaurant business. His brother, Israel Witron, runs the growing Bigo's Bistro on Watson Boulevard in Warner Robins. Check out The Back Burner, located in the quaint Ingleside area, and get a taste of this creative chef's work.

CRAB CAKES

INGREDIENTS

1 pound crab meat
1/2 red bell pepper, *diced*
1 lemon, *juiced*
2 tablespoons breadcrumbs
1/4 cup vegetable oil
3 green onions, *diced*
1/4 teaspoon Old Bay
1/2 cup mayo

PREPARATION

Combine all ingredients—except crab meat and vegetable oil—in a large bowl, using spatula to gently stir until just combined. Using the spatula, add the crab meat, making sure to keep large chunks. With your hands, create balls of the mixture and set aside.

Heat vegetable oil in a pan over a low flame. Once the oil is hot, place a ball into the pan. Cook about three minutes on low.

Using a spatula, gently press the top of the ball to give it shape and flip over. Cook an additional three minutes on low.

Serve with lemon wedge or your favorite sauce.

AVOCADO PICO DE GALLO DIP

INGREDIENTS

4 avocados, *diced*
1 medium red onion, *diced*
1 tablespoon white vinegar
1 bunch cilantro, *chopped*
1 large jalapeño
seeded and diced
2 limes, *juiced*
4 Roma tomatoes, *diced*
Salt and Pepper
Salt and pepper
1 teaspoon garlic
finely chopped

PREPARATION

In a mixing bowl, combine roma tomatoes, cilantro, red onion, jalapeño, white vinegar, garlic, lime juice, salt and pepper. Once mixed, stir in the avocados. Serve with your favorite tortilla chips or as the perfect topping for grilled steak, fish, or chicken.

Dicing an avacado *Using a sharp knife, halve the avocado and remove the seed. Cut a grid pattern into the avocado half, cutting down and then sideways to form "squares." Be careful not to pierce through the outside skin of the avocado. Using a large spoon, scoop out the diced avocado by running the spoon edge between the skin and the meat of the avocado.*

AWARD WINNING TRES LECHES CAKE

INGREDIENTS

24 ounces lemon wedge cookies *dusted with powdered sugar and finely ground*

1 cup flour

1 1/2 cup sugar

7 eggs

4 tablespoons baking powder

2 cans condensed milk

2 cans evaporated milk

2 cups regular milk

PREPARATION

Preheat oven to 350 degrees. Combine the condensed milk, evaporated milk and regular milk and refrigerate.

Combine the eggs and sugar. Beat with electric mixer until the mixture turns a light yellow and is fluffy. Add the finely ground cookie crumbs and baking powder little by little while continuing to use the electric mixer. Bake for 35-40 minutes.

As soon as the cake comes out of the oven, pour the milk mixture over the top and place in the refrigerator for one hour. Top with chantilly cream.

This recipe won the 2016 Girl Scouts of Historic Georgia Cookie Competition. For the competition, Chef Rosas used the Savannah Smiles Girl Scout Cookies.

Chris Barton and Cesare Mammarella

BEARFOOT TAVERN
AND GASTRO PUB

BILLED AS MACON AND CENTRAL GEORGIA'S ONLY GASTRO PUB AND BEER GARDEN, Bearfoot Tavern on Second Street downtown is one more of the Hotplates Restaurant Group. This one, like the others, is getting excellent reviews.

Entering Bearfoot's front door, one encounters a friendly greeting and a spacious bar area with ample booth and bar-side seating for a crowd. A huge television screen is overhead, likely showing football or some other game, and the bartenders are accommodating, quick, and friendly.

Those who are there for dinner may walk past the bar and into the large but cozy dining area. There's also a private dining room and lovely 40- to 50-seat beer garden at the back of the property. All totaled, there's room for 150 patrons.

Moving from an older, smaller space into more room for dining plus a larger kitchen provided a lot of options," said owner Cesare Mammarella. "We re-did the entire menu," he said. "We wanted to gear the menu and the atmosphere to middle-aged couples and families, and this building was easily arranged so that we were able to serve more people and they can enjoy the meal without noise. We also have a bigger kitchen."

The dining area is located so that there is no noise coming from the bar. A new brick oven has been installed for pizza-making, and, Cesare added, "We now do an eight-ounce burger on the grill that people love. In addition, we have 50 draft beers on tap now, and almost half are from Georgia breweries."

According to Chris Barton, Bearfoot tries to use as much local and regional produce, getting vegetables the day after they are picked. The kitchen staff takes advantage of a farmer's market on Wesleyan Drive and other area farms for fresh vegetables. "There are farmers all over Georgia and in Florida who raise good vegetables for sale," Cesare said.

Chris Barton, who began as a server and moved up to General Manager, was promoted to Director of Operations for Hotplates Group prior to the opening of the new Bearfoot Tavern. "Chris was an integral part of the design of the new space, as well as our fifty-draft system that was designed and constructed specifically for Bearfoot," said Cesare.

And in case you're wondering what a Gastro Pub is, Cesare explained, "It's an old English/Irish term for public house, gastro coming from gastronomy, meaning fine food," he said. "It's a place to enjoy fine food and beer."

CHICKEN PESTO PIZZA

INGREDIENTS

3 ounces cherry tomatoes
cut in quarters

3 ounces roasted red peppers
julienne

6 ounces baked chicken breast
shredded

4 ounces fresh mozzarella cheese
drained and crumbled

Pizza dough of choice

10 pieces garlic

3/4 cup pine nuts, *toasted*

1 cup lemon juice

1 tablespoon kosher salt

1/2 cup parmesan cheese

1 cup vegetable oil

1/2 cup extra virgin olive oil

PREPARATION

Preheat oven to 500 degrees.

Combine garlic, pine nuts, lemon juice, kosher salt, parmesan cheese, and oils in food processor to make a pesto.

Stretch out your favorite store bought pizza dough to 14-inch on a preheated pizza stone.

Evenly spread 3 ounces of the homemade pesto to the edges of the dough.

Toss the remaining pesto and chicken together and top pizza with tossed chicken, tomatoes, peppers and cheese.

Bake for approximately 6 minutes or until dough edges are crispy.

ASIAN SALAD

INGREDIENTS

4 ounces cooked lo mein noodles
May omit noodles.

2 ounces baby spinach, *chiffonade*

2 ounces carrots, *julienne*

2 ounces salted peanuts, *chopped*

1 tablespoon cilantro, *chiffonade*

1 teaspoon mint, *chiffonade*

2 ounces mandarin orange segments, *drained*

6 ounces grilled chicken breast *chopped*

2 cups soy sauce

1 cup water

1 cup rice wine vinegar

1 3/4 cups honey

1/4 cup Dijon mustard

1 tablespoon ginger, *minced*

1/4 cup sesame oil

2 1/4 cups vegetable oil

PREPARATION

Mix soy sauce, water, rice wine vinegar, honey, Dijon mustard, and ginger and blend well.

Continue blending while slowly adding the sesame oil and vegetable oil to the mixture until it emulsifies to make a sesame ginger dressing. *Keep cool in the fridge until ready to use.*

Mix together all other ingredients in bowl and toss with 4 ounces of the sesame ginger dressing.

Serves 1

Dressing yields 2 quarts

BRASSERIE CIRCA

BRASSERIE CIRCA'S CHARMING ATMOSPHERE HAS MADE IT A FAVORED PLACE TO GO, whether for a meal or simply for a drink and conversation. Part of the Hotplates Restaurant Group in Macon, Brasserie Circa is one of many establishments owned by Cesare Mammarella. Since opening in August of 2013, the restaurant's relaxed setting and friendly, casual atmosphere, reminiscent of a French or European café, continues to draw a crowd of first-timers who often become regular customers.

"We're very proud of all the regulars who come in, and we know them by their first and last names," said Brasserie Circa's General Manager Chelsea Leverett. "This is a friendly neighborhood restaurant, a nice little spot where people can come and feel comfortable."

Also a major draw is the excellent choice of foods prepared by Head Chef Roberto Del Cid Posada. The menu features classic and contemporary French and European cuisine and from day to day may offer quite a variety, such as steaks, pasta, large salads, sushi and more. A world traveler, Chef Posada is known for his sushi, steaks and what has been called "a phenomenal salmon dish."

Brasserie Circa's dining room is open for lunch and dinner and seats as many as ninety people. There is also a private room available for parties as large as thirty. Additionally, wooden pergolas strung with bistro lights offer diners a quiet and romantic setting for dinner or just a cocktail.

On any given day or night, it's best to make a reservation to dine at this quaint restaurant as seating tends to fill up fast. If you do visit, make sure to ask for a Ruthy Sangria. Ruthy, a Brasserie Circa and Rebuilding Macon alum, provided the restaurant with a knock your socks off sangria recipe. It is made by the glass and diners have the choice of red or white, so you can pick your preference.

Roberto Del Cid Posada

LA CREMA
SONOMA COAST
2013 PINOT NOIR

STEAK EMERSON

INGREDIENTS

2, 5- to 10-ounce steak filets
1 cup extra virgin olive oil
1/2 cup shallots
1 1/2 tablespoons honey
1 tablespoon thyme, *chopped*
1 tablespoon rosemary, *chopped*
Season with salt and pepper

PREPARATION

Combine all ingredients in bowl and add filets to marinade. Let sit, chilled, for 24 hours.

Grill to desired temperature (medium-rare is recommended).

Serve with farm-fresh vegetables and mashed potatoes.

Serves 2

HAWAIIAN LOBSTER ROLL

INGREDIENTS

2 cups sushi rice, *yields 4 cups*
4 nori sheets
2 cups cooked lobster tail meat
1 avocado, *sliced into thin pieces*
1 cup fresh mango *chopped*
1 cup cucumber *slivered into thin pieces*
1 cup flour
1 tablespoon cornstarch
1 1/2 cups seltzer water
Oil for frying
Sesame seeds for garnish
Soy sauce for dipping

PREPARATION

RICE Wash rice at least 3 times or until water is clear. Fill rice cooker or large pot with water to about 1-inch over rice.

In a small bowl combine vinegar, sugar, and salt and microwave for 30-45 seconds. Transfer the rice into a large wooden or glass mixing bowl and add the vinegar mixture. Fold thoroughly to combine and coat each grain of rice with the mixture. Allow to cool to room temperature before using to make sushi.

TEMPURA To make tempura batter, combine flour, cornstarch, seltzer water, and salt in bowl and mix well.

Heat oil in pan on medium heat. Coat lobster tail pieces in batter and fry in skillet. Let pieces rest on paper towels to drain oil.

SUSHI ROLL Lay out Nori sheet on table and evenly top with sushi rice. Lay pieces of fried lobster, mango, and cucumber on top of rice. Roll nori sheet tight and lay avocado across top, covering entire roll.

Slice roll into 6-8 pieces and garnish with sesame seeds.

Dip in soy sauce.

Makes 4 rolls

Pino Mauro and Don Biving

BURKE MANSION

"THERE'S A NICE THING ABOUT A BED AND BREAKFAST. It's like having friends in the house all the time," said Don Bivings, who with co-owner Pino Mauro, runs the Burke Mansion B&B on Georgia Avenue. "Our guests are incredible; it's like each one is a new friend."

The two men moved to Macon from Las Vegas in 2006 and at first opened Market City Café downtown. Their real wish was to dedicate themselves full time to operating their new home as a B&B. They had purchased and installed elegant furnishings, and the old Mansion's beauty could not be ignored.

When they closed the café they "went full steam," Mr. Bivings said. They advertised the mansion nationally and on March 19, 2016, received their first guests.

"And of the guests we've had, only two had ever stopped in Macon before," Mr. Bivings said. Their guests have come not only from many parts of this country but from Belgium, Germany, England and Italy too.

"We pop up all the time as a No. 1 rated B&B, with five stars—and part of it is we offer a different level of service from the others," Mr. Bivings said. "We have high-end amenities—1,200-thread-count sheets, down comforters—what you would expect from a high-end hotel."

Only three bedrooms at a time are open, which limits the house to six or eight guests. Meals are served on snowy white tablecloths in the dining room on Wedgewood Napoleon Ivy china with sterling and crystal, or on a tray in a guest's room if the guest prefers. A full complement of morning foods is served at breakfast, including goodies such as French toast.

One visitor described the breakfast "like breakfast at Downton Abbey." Mr. Bivings terms it "jaw-dropping." Mr. Mauro, the mansion's chef, refers to himself as "chief cook and bottle-washer" and jokes that he is the sole chef, "because our kitchen isn't large enough for both of us."

When a guest checks in, they are asked to choose preference of times to dine so that meals can suit their plans. If guests wish to dine out, "We will drive them to their dinner spot," Mr. Bivings said.

Dessert is offered in the evening and there is a library where guests can relax and read.

Guests are awed by the size of the large rooms and by the original elevator with its wire walls that allow those being transported to see the ride from the inside out as they go up or down.

The house was built for the Burke family in 1887, and the family lived there until the mid-1960s. In excellent condition, the house remains much as it was in its early days.

FRENCH TOAST NAPOLEON

INGREDIENTS

8 one-inch slices of egg-bread *such as challah or brioche*

CUSTARD

2 cups heavy cream
1 large egg
2 teaspoons ground cinnamon

CHANTILLY CREAM

2 cups heavy cream
1 teaspoon vanilla
1 cup powdered sugar
2 cups fresh mixed berries, *sliced*

PREPARATION

Place the sliced egg bread in the freezer making sure it is frozen.

CUSTARD Mix the heavy cream, large egg, and cinnamon in a bowl and chill for at least 1 hour.

CREAM In a separate bowl, use a hand mixer to thoroughly mix the heavy cream, vanilla, and 3/4 cup powdered sugar.

Start on the lowest speed and gradually work up to the highest speed. The mixture will become fluffy like whipped cream.

Heat a skillet on medium heat and use a non-stick spray before each batch.

Press each slice of bread into the custard being careful to not oversoak. Cook the soaked bread in a skillet until golden brown, about 4 minutes on each side.

To assemble, layer each piece of toast with a chantilly cream dollop and fresh berries, continuing to layer another piece of toast.

Dust with the remaining powdered sugar and serve with warm syrup of choice.

Serves 4

PARIS
SPAIN

PICKLED EGG SALAD CROSTINI
WITH PROSCIUTTO AND HOMEMADE MAYONNAISE

INGREDIENTS

1/2 cup apple cider vinegar
1/2 cup distilled white vinegar
1/3 cup mayonnaise
1 teaspoon sugar
1 1/2 teaspoon kosher salt
6 large eggs
2 tablespoons parsley *finely chopped*
2 tablespoons chives *finely chopped*
12 quarter-inch sliced country style bread *such as ciabatta or baguette*
3 tablespoons olive oil
2 garlic cloves
12 pieces prosciutto
Salt and pepper to taste
Soft parsley leaves for serving

MAYONNAISE

1 1/2 tablespoons white wine vinegar
1 tablespoon Dijon mustard
1/2 teaspoon salt
1 large egg
2 cups canola oil

PREPARATION

Bring vinegars, sugar, salt, and water to a boil. Let cool.

Place eggs in a medium saucepan and add water to cover by 2 inches. Bring to a boil, cover, and remove from heat. Let sit 10 minutes.

Transfer eggs to a bowl of ice water to cool. Drain, peel, and return to bowl.

Add cooled pickling liquid, cover and refrigerate at least 12 hours.

Mix the white wine vinegar, Dijon mustard, salt, and large egg. Slowly add the canola oil until the mixture emulsifies into a mayonnaise. *You may refrigerate for up to 1 month. Makes 2 1/2 cups.*

Remove eggs from pickling liquid. Coarsely chop the eggs and mix with homemade mayonnaise, chives, and parsley in a medium bowl. Season with salt and pepper and some pickling liquid if desired. Chill until ready to serve.

Preheat oven to 425 degrees.

Place bread on baking sheet and drizzle with olive oil. Toast until golden brown, 5-8 minutes. Rub with garlic and top each piece with pickled egg salad, parsley, and a slice of prosciutto.

Egg salad serves 12

EDGAR'S BISTRO

EDGAR'S BISTRO IS THRIVING as Helms College's first autonomous restaurant in Macon.

Situated just across Eisenhower Parkway from the Middle Georgia State University campus and adjacent to the Anderson Conference Center, the Bistro has become a favorite dining destination for those who have discovered its location, tempting menus, and the friendly service of its student staff.

Both Edgar's Bistro and Helms College are named for Dr. Edgar J. Helms, founder of Goodwill Industries. Both of these entities are present on the site and, along with the Anderson Conference Center, are under the policy and administrative guidance of Goodwill Industries of Middle Georgia and the Central Savannah River Area (CSRA).

Chef Stuart Hardy, from Grand Rapids, Michigan, came to Helms College in 2012 as an adjunct instructor. He serves as the Bistro's Executive Chef now and also ranks as the Assistant Department Chair for Helms College Macon campus. The college supported Chef Hardy's suggestion of allowing students to gain firsthand learning in the kitchen and dining room by becoming an entirely student-run restaurant. The idea has been a great success for all involved.

"Real experiential learning makes this school unique from all others," Chef Hardy said. "Students enjoy practicing their trade for real customers who have the opportunity to provide feedback to chefs in training."

The Bistro menu changes quarterly and can be found online. Recently, it offered such inviting dishes from the garden as a Grilled Chicken and Strawberry Pecan Salad, a Seared Duck with Honey & Fig Salad, and Warm Spinach Chorizo Salad. Just two of several entrées shown were the Southern Fried Pork Chops and Lobster Risotto. The risotto is made from scratch using student-prepared fresh lobster stock and is accompanied by a plump Main lobster tail. Tempting appetizers are student crafted with the guidance of a trained, professionally certified chef.

Customer reviews are quite complimentary. One termed the Bistro "a hidden gem" and another declares, "Can't wait to go back again." Prices are reasonable, and the restaurant truly strives to impress its guests. Chef Hardy said that the dining room is drawing a growing number of new and repeat customers, "Word of mouth is everything," he said.

Stuart Hardy

SNAPPER
WITH MANGO CHUTNEY

INGREDIENTS

2 snapper fillets, *skin on*
1 teaspoon salad oil
1 teaspoon fresh ginger, *grated*
Salt and Pepper

MANGO CHUTNEY

1 1/2 cup mango, *diced*
1/4 cup red onion, *diced*
1/4 cup red bell pepper, *diced*
1/2 cup cilantro, *chopped*
1 jalapeño, *minced*
1 lime, *juiced*
Salt

PREPARATION

CHUTNEY In a small bowl, stir together jalapeño and lime juice. Set aside for 5 minutes.

In a separate bowl, mix the diced mango, red onion, cilantro, and pepper.

Combine both bowls and incorporate well. Season with salt and additional lime juice.

FISH Score the skin of the snapper in a diamond shape being careful not to cut the flesh. Rub the fish with oil and season lightly with ginger, salt, and pepper.

Turn the broiler to high and allow to heat fully.

Put the fish on a sheet tray and place in a hot broiler until light browning on edges of skin occurs and fish becomes fork tender.

Serve over jasmine rice with chutney, lime wedge, and cilantro for garnish.

Serves 2

DUCK
WITH VALENCIA ORANGE GASTRIQUE

INGREDIENTS

2 farm-raised duck breasts

1 teaspoon salad oil

Salt and pepper

GLAZE

1 Valencia orange
juiced and zested

1/2 cup red wine vinegar or rice wine vinegar

1/2 cup granulated sugar

1 teaspoon water

Pinch of salt

PREPARATION

GLAZE Zest orange skin into thick strands and add to a small pot of boiling water for 2 minutes. Drain the water and put orange zest in ice bath to cool.

Mix the sugar with 1 teaspoon of water in a small pot over medium-high heat for 5 minutes until the water evaporates and sugar begins to caramelize. Once sugar is completely melted, carefully add vinegar and stir for 2 more minutes. Pour in orange juice, pinch of salt, and blanched orange zest to simmer for an additional 5 minutes until reduced to thick syrup.

DUCK Score the skin of the duck in a diamond pattern being careful not to cut the flesh. Rub the duck with oil and season lightly with salt and pepper.

Heat sauté pan to medium-high heat and add the duck skin side down and cover. Keep the duck in the pan skin side down until the fat has rendered down about 8 minutes. Flip the duck and increase the heat. Cook for 2 minutes uncovered.

Pour the melted fat off into a container and flip the duck back to skin side down to crisp the skin. Slice the duck on a bias and pour warm gastrique over the top. Serve with mashed potatoes or risotto and garnish with orange zest and parsley.

Serves 2

SEARED SCALLOP
WITH GINGER CARROT PURÉE

INGREDIENTS

12 large diver scallops
1 teaspoon olive oil
2 tablespoons melted butter
Salt and Pepper

CARROT PURÉE

1 tablespoon canola oil
1 teaspoon sesame oil
2 tablespoons shallots, *chopped*
2 cups chicken stock
2 cups young carrot *peeled and diced*
1 tablespoon soy sauce
1 tablespoon fresh ginger *peeled and grated*
1 tablespoon rice wine vinegar
1 tablespoon honey

PREPARATION

PURÉE Heat the canola oil in a saucepan over low heat and sweat the shallots until tender. Add the stock and bring to a boil.

Stir in the carrots and reduce the heat to simmer until the carrots are just tender. Reserve the broth.

Add the carrots to a blender and add the soy sauce, ginger, rice wine vinegar, honey, and sesame oil. Purée the ingredients until smooth, adding the broth back while blender is on until desired consistency is achieved.

Press through strainer with rubber spatula and discard the solids in strainer.

SCALLOPS Rinse the scallops under cold water and pat dry.

Lightly season with salt and pepper and sauté in oiled pan on high. Leave undisturbed for 2 minutes or until bottom has evenly browned.

Flip scallops carefully and lower heat. Add melted butter to the pan.

Remove from the heat and pour sauce on plate. Serve with sugar snapped peas.

Serves 2

EL CAMINO

COY GREGORY IS A MACON NATIVE who developed his cooking skills while he was a student at Valdosta State College. Today, he is general manager of El Camino Taqueria and Cantina, a thriving Mexican restaurant and bar on Second Street, just around the corner from Cherry Street in downtown Macon.

El Camino opened in March 2016 during the annual Cherry Blossom Festival. With crowds of local residents downtown and also many out-of-town visitors there, it was an opportune time for a new eatery to appear on the scene.

"The festival gave us lots of exposure," Mr. Gregory said with a grin. "We got lots of exposure, and we made lots and lots of tacos."

The El Camino menu offers five different tacos including a steak taco and a fish taco, served up with a fresh, smoky taste. That fresh, smoky taste is what makes El Camino's smoked meats its biggest seller, Mr. Gregory said.

In addition, El Camino offers the traditional Mexican sides: refried beans, cheese grits, Mexican rice, and Mexican Street Corn—that's corn on the cob, roasted with seasonings and spices and served hot.

"The food we provide is excellent quality, with meat smoked fresh every day and prepared right at the back door," he said. "It goes straight from smoker to kitchen to table."

El Camino also offers tortas—sandwiches—of which the most popular are the Bandito, a short-rib sandwich, and the Alberto, a smoked chicken sandwich. Wings are smoked fresh every day and served with buffalo sauce, "and they are top-notch," Mr. Gregory said. Other sidebar treats include lettuce, tomato and guacamole, a jalapeño radish slaw, and cotija cheese, and everything is topped off with crema, a sauce something like sour cream.

"We also do salads and chips and dips, and Kitchen Manager Josh Abshire comes up with specials every day," Mr. Gregory said.

A big advantage for El Camino is its proximity to the Cox Capitol Theater next door. "On show nights, we're really busy for dinner," he said. "We complement the music scene in downtown Macon. Music shows are our best nights. Bragg Jam at the end of July ought to be huge."

The El Camino kitchen connects to the Cox Capitol Theater lobby, "so we can sell through there," Mr. Gregory said. "That really drives our business on show nights. On those nights, we're jam-packed."

Coy Gregory

MEXICAN RICE

INGREDIENTS

8 cups rice
16 cups water
2 cups white onion, *finely diced*
1 cup celery, *finely diced*
1 teaspoon ground cumin
4 tablespoons kosher salt
1 teaspoon black pepper
3 tablespoons tomato paste
3 tablespoons Pasilla Negra chili powder

PREPARATION

Place rice in large cooking pot.

Thoroughly combine all other ingredients.

Combine rice and mixture in large cooking pot.

Bring to a boil, lower heat, and cook 20 minutes or until tender.

Serves 24

TOASTED PUMPKIN SEED AND PINTO HUMMUS

INGREDIENTS

8 cups pinto beans, *cooked*
2 cups pumpkin seeds, *toasted*
1/2 cup lemon juice
2 1/2 tablespoons kosher salt
2 tablespoons black pepper

PREPARATION

Add all ingredients in a large blender, combine until smooth in texture.

Serve with choice of crackers, chips, or vegetables.

SALSA VERDE

INGREDIENTS

4 cans whole tomatillas, drained
6 cups white onions
8 garlic bulbs
8 cups reserved tomatilla liquid
1 cup lime juice
1 cup cilantro
3 tablespoons salt
2 tablespoons pepper

PREPARATION

Preheat oven to 400 degrees.

Strain tomatillos and reserve liquid for later. Roast tomatillos, white onions, and garlic bulbs until golden brown, about 20 minutes.

Combine in large blender with the rest of the ingredients. Mix thoroughly and serve cold with favorite tortilla chips.

Natasha Philli

FOUNTAIN OF JUICE

NATASHA AND CARL PHILLIPS FIRST OPENED Fountain of Juice as a smoothie and juice bar in about 700 square feet of space just off Vineville Avenue.

When they added salads and sandwiches to the menu, word spread, more customers came, and the business "just kind of took off," Natasha said. Though they were able to double their tiny restaurant's space to accommodate some additional diners, they still needed more room.

In November 2014, they found the answer. A much larger area became available The space would accommodate many diners and enable the couple to install upgrades they had dreamed of, including additional staff. And so, they moved.

"The opportunity came, the landlords are friends of ours, and it was really good timing," Natasha said.

Besides the spacious main dining room, a sizeable side room accommodates an overflow of diners or a private party. The restaurant's employees number 32—a big jump from the "maybe eight" helpers at the original site, she said. "And we have some employees who've worked with my mom for fifteen years."

From childhood, Natasha has been familiar with food preparation and the restaurant business. She is the daughter of Natalia Del Basso Orsini, known throughout Georgia and beyond for her own Macon restaurant, Natalia's. And while Natasha's husband, Carl, is probably best known for his art, he has proven himself to be an artist in the kitchen as well. On an early morning, he may be found preparing the Chicken Salad that Natasha said has gained wide admiration.

The menu itself is amazing, offering more than a dozen lunch time "starters," plus quiches, sandwiches, entrees and burgers. The Saturday brunch includes mimosas as well as a range of midday selections.

"The chicken salad and pimento cheese, our cold plate, has taken off, and our burgers have done really well," Natasha said.

The wide choice of entrees served after 5 p.m. includes such customer favorites as Petite Filet with Fried Green Tomatoes and Candied Bacon. Other suppertime faves include Sea Bass Tacos, Pecan Encrusted Grouper, a wide selection of pastas and sides, and much more.

Fountain of Juice offers catering, including party hors d'oeuvres for pickup or delivery. There are even special drinks for those feeling a need to detox.

With two generations of talented restaurateurs in the family, it is also possible that there might be a third generation of culinary genius coming along. Natasha and Carl have two sons, Salvador, age 9, and Roman, age 7. Salvador is into sports, his mom said, but "Roman is a foodie. He already wants to prepare his own food."

BUTTERNUT SQUASH LASAGNA

INGREDIENTS

3 pounds roasted butternut squash
1 sweet onion, *finely diced*
1 clove garlic, *minced*
3 leaves fresh sage, *chopped*
3 tablespoons butter
Salt and pepper to taste

SAUCE

3 tablespoons butter
1 clove garlic
4 tablespoons flour
5 cups warm milk
1 bay leaf
1 teaspoon salt
Pepper
1/4 cup fresh parmesan

ASSEMBLY

1/2 pound fresh mozzarella, *cubed*
1 cup fresh parmesan
1/2 cup hazelnuts *chopped and lightly toasted*
Box of no boil lasagna noodles

PREPARATION

Sauté onion in butter until translucent. Add garlic and cook until fragrant and then add squash, sage, and salt and pepper. Mix well and allow to cool.

Using a non-reactive pot, sauté garlic in butter until fragrant, then add flour and cook until lightly golden. On medium heat, add milk, bay leaf, salt and pepper and whisk away. Keep whisking until mixture boils, reduce heat and whisk until it thickens into a sauce and coats the back of a spoon. Once finished, remove bay leaf, add parmesan and mix well.

Assemble lasagna in pan by adding sauce first, then noodles, then squash mixture, then 1/4 pound mozzarella, 1/3 cup parmesan, then top with more sauce, noodles, squash, rest of mozzarella, 1/3 cup parmesan, sauce, noodles, rest of sauce, rest of parmesan and hazelnuts. Cover with foil and cook in oven about 30 minutes. Uncover for 15-20 minutes until bubbling.

Allow lasagna to rest for 15 minutes before slicing.

Serves 10

NILLA NILLA CUPCAKES

INGREDIENTS

1 cup cake flour
2 cups sugar
3/4 teaspoon salt
4 large eggs

2 cups all-purpose flour
1 tablespoon baking powder
1 cup unsalted butter, *cubed*
1 cup 2% milk
1 tablespoon pure vanilla extract

PREPARATION

Preheat oven to 325 degrees.

Line pans with paper liners and set aside.

In the bowl of an electric mixer fitted with the paddle attachment, combine flours, sugar, baking powder, and salt. Mix on low speed until combined. Add butter, mixing until just coated with flour.

Whisk together the eggs, vanilla, and milk in a bowl.

With mixer on medium speed, add wet ingredients in 3 additions, scraping down sides of bowl before each. Mix until just incorporated.

Divide batter evenly among liners, filling about 2/3 full.

Bake, rotating pan halfway through until cake tester inserted in center comes out clean (about 17-20 minutes).

Transfer to a wire rack to cool completely. Once cupcakes have cooled, top with your favorite icing and enjoy.

Makes 30 cupcakes

GREY GOOSE PLAYER'S CLUB

Joe Hernandez's parents are from Cuba and, as is somewhat traditional among Cubans, Joe's mother made him learn to cook at an early age.

"I found I enjoyed it," he said. "I liked experimenting with foods."

Now owner of the Grey Goose Players Club for the past 11 years, Hernandez is still experimenting with foods and with cooking, and he meets with his chef twice a week to plan various specials for the Club's menu.

Some of his longtime customers are aware of his interest in foods, and sometimes some of them bring him dishes to try out.

"If I like a dish, I name it and put it on the menu," he said, "like our parmesan encrusted shrimp, or chicken over a linguini bed, or our sun-dried tomato cream sauce—all came straight from one of our customers."

The Grey Goose has a warm and cozy feel, and Hernandez works to keep it that way. "I have been blessed with repeat business. It's sort of like a meeting place for friends, a family tavern atmosphere. My servers know you and they know what you want. We're a place where locals plan to go.

"We get couples, families, grandparents with grandchildren. I really have a diverse group," he said. "We try to get to know the customers and learn what they like. We're famous for our Gooseburgers (really a half pound of ground chuck), our fresh seafood platters, and our hand-cut steaks."

Many customers, especially the children, get a big kick out of watching the colorful fish that swim in the large freshwater and saltwater tanks separating the dining room from the bar.

"Our fish tanks are a huge draw with the kids," Hernandez said.

A few long-time patrons have adopted a favorite seat in the dining room or at the bar, where they have sat during their visits over the years. In several cases, Hernandez has had small brass plaques placed on each of these spots bearing the "owner's" name. "They really enjoy having their "own" seat," he said.

Hernandez attributes a large part of the Goose's success to great employees—who feel like family. Also with a seasoned staff, including some long-time favorites, several actual family members contribute to the close-knit atmosphere. Joe and Sonia, his wife, have two sons—ages 13 and 16—who are learning the ropes of the restaurant business. Joe's mother-in-law, Miss Bobbie, frequently works at the Goose. "I think she's more popular than me," Hernandez says.

The bottom line is that the Grey Goose is a family affair, and that's just the way Joe likes it.

aime Lucas and Joe Hernandez

CHARLESTON MAC N' CHEESE

INGREDIENTS

2 tablespoons olive oil

2 tablespoons butter, *melted*

1/2 onion, *finely minced*

1 pound lump crab meat
may substitute in 1/2 pound shrimp

1 pound sea shell pasta

4 tablespoons flour

2 cups heavy cream

1 pound mascarpone cheese

TOPPING

2 cloves of minced garlic

3/4 cup panko

2 tablespoons olive oil

1 tablespoon parsley
chopped

1 tablespoon chives
finely chopped

3 tablespoons parmesan cheese
shredded

Salt and pepper to taste

PREPARATION

Melt butter in saucepan. Add minced onion and sauté 2-4 minutes.

Add crab meat and sauté 1 to 2 minutes and set aside.

Cook pasta according to package directions.

Melt 2 tablespoons butter and two tablespoons of olive oil in saucepan. Slowly whisk in flour, being careful not to burn.

Slowly whisk in heavy cream until sauce thickens. Mix in mascarpone. Remove from heat.

Mix in crab mixture and pasta. Place in individual ramekins or casserole dish. Set aside.

Mix topping ingredients together. Sprinkle over pasta. Broil till golden brown.

Serves 4 to 6

EGGPLANT FRIES
WITH BASIL AIOLI

Serves 2 to 4

INGREDIENTS

1 large eggplant
2 cups Italian breadcrumbs
1 1/2 tablespoon black pepper
1 cup flour
2 tablespoons salt
1 can evaporated milk

AIOLI

1 cup mayo
1 lemon, *juiced*
Salt and pepper to taste
3 tablespoons fresh basil, *chopped*

PREPARATION

AIOLI Whisk the mayo, basil, lemon juice, salt, and pepper together and chill in fridge until needed.

FRIES Peel and cut eggplant into fries. Mix flour, breadcrumbs, salt, and pepper together in shallow bowl.

Place evaporated milk in separate bowl. Preheat canola oil in heavy fry pan over medium high heat.

In batches, dip fries in milk, then flour mixture to coat thoroughly. Fry in batches till golden brown and serve with basil aioli for dipping.

SUMMER GOOSE SLIDERS

INGREDIENTS

2 pounds ground chuck

1 green bell pepper
finely chopped

Lettuce

3 tablespoons garlic, *minced*

3 tablespoons soy sauce

3 tablespoons Worcestershire

Salt and pepper to taste

1 egg

1 medium onion
finely chopped

Tomato slices

Slider buns or rolls

1 cup mayo

1 tablespoon garlic salt

1/2 pound pepper jack cheese slices

3 tablespoons chipotle adobo sauce

Serves 6 to 8

PREPARATION

Mix mayo, chipotle sauce, and garlic salt together and refrigerate until needed.

Mix meat with egg, pepper, onion, and garlic, soy sauce, and Worcestershire sauce. Form into small, slider-sized patties. Place patties on hot grill or pan sear in hot non-stick skillet. Flip only once and top with cheese. Remove from heat once cheese melts.

Assemble sliders starting with chipotle mayo, patty, lettuce and tomato.

GRITS CAFÉ

THE VERY POPULAR GRITS CAFÉ on the courthouse square in downtown Forsyth opened in 1999, and café owner Wayne Wetendorf gives his staff much of the credit for the café's widespread popularity.

The Café seats 160 diners and draws local customers as well as repeat customers from surrounding counties and beyond. On Fridays and Saturdays there's likely to be a wait list for seating. "That's quite a feat in a town of this size," Mr. Wetendorf said. "It says a lot about my team."

During holiday seasons, many repeat travelers making long journeys on Interstate 75 stop in to dine at the café and swap holiday greetings with Mr. Wetendorf and the staff.

The Grits Café employees are a close-knit group, much like a family. "We treat each other with respect," Mr. Wetendorf said. "We're positive, motivated and upbeat. I'm very fortunate to have such a fabulous team."

Leslie Waters is dining room manager and her husband, Jamie Waters, has charge of the kitchen, where the café's delicious food is prepared daily from scratch. Locally grown vegetables come from the nearby Watson Farms and the Forsyth Farmers Market, and the staff reaches out to other growers as well. Grassroots Farms in Tattnall County is one farm that supplies pork sausage, bacon, and country ham.

"We're small business owners, so we strive to support other small businesses in and around Monroe County," Mr. Wetendorf said.

A charcuterie program features local sausage, bacon, and country ham. The sausage, bacon, and hams are smoked in-house, and many times peach tree wood from Dickey Farms in Musella has been used for this process. Once the meats are smoked, sous chefs Ben Banks and Chad Smith use the fragrant meats to create delights such as fresh potato chips with a hint of bacon or barbecue rub. The treats complement the café's ever-changing full bar and also its martini menu.

To top off the delicious meals, Grits has been working to increase their dessert options.

"Our team is doing an amazing job of picking out desserts for the menu," Mr. Wetendorf said. New desserts include Hummingbird Cake, a tasty treasure from the Caribbean islands, and another called Muddy Baked Alaska. Both are quite popular with the café's regular diners. Just how popular? Wayne put it this way: "We have one guest who begins his meal with a dessert."

amie Waters

SPICY GARLIC-DILL QUICKLES

INGREDIENTS

1 1/2 quarts cucumbers, *sliced*

5 1/2 garlic cloves, *smashed*

2 tablespoons crushed red pepper

2 tablespoons dill seed

PICKLING BRINE

1 quart apple cider vinegar

1/2 quart water

1/2 quart sugar

6 tablespoons salt

PREPARATION

Slice cucumbers and combine with smashed garlic, crushed red pepper, and dill seed in a 4-quart container.

In a sauce pot, bring apple cider vinegar, water, sugar, and salt to a boil. Stir until sugar is dissolved and pour over the cucumbers. Let cool uncovered at room temperature and enjoy.

Makes 4 quarts

GRIT'S MARTINI
WITH SHIITAKE CREAM SAUCE

INGREDIENTS

3 cups shrimp stock
1 1/2 cups cream
1/4 tablespoon chicken base
1 cup grits
1/2 tablespoon salt and pepper
4 tablespoons butter

CREAM SAUCE

1/2 quart shiitake stems
1 ounce butter
1/4 quart water
3/4 quart cream
1 1/4 tablespoon
1 1/4 tablespoon plus 1/4 teaspoon water
1 teaspoon salt and pepper plus 1/4 teaspoon cornstarch

TOPPING

Small bunch parsley *chopped*
5 pieces bacon *cooked and chopped*
30 shrimp *peeled and deveined*

PREPARATION

Combine stock, cream, chicken base, salt, pepper, grits, and butter in large pot and cook over low heat until desired consistency is reached.

Preheat oven to 425 degrees.

Toss shiitake stems in melted butter and roast for 12 minutes.

Put roasted stems in a medium size stock pot, add water and bring to a boil. Reduce to a simmer until water is reduced by half. Strain through a fine sieve, rinse pot.

Return to the pot and add in cream, bring to a boil, reduce and simmer. Reduce by half once again.

Combine the cornstarch and water, add to pot and stir to thicken. Bring sauce back to a boil to cook out the corn starch. Season to taste.

Sauté shrimp in buttered pan.

FINISH Fill martini glass with 4 ounces of grits and layer 1-2 ounces shiitake cream sauce on top. Chop 2 pieces of shrimp in half and layer on top of cream. Sprinkle each martini with bacon pieces and parsley. Hang remaining shrimp off the side of each martini as a garnish.

Serves 10

STICKY TOFFEE CAKE

INGREDIENTS

12 pitted dried dates

3/4 cup fresh brewed coffee, plus 1 teaspoon

1/2 teaspoon baking soda

1/4 teaspoon vanilla extract

5 tablespoons butter

2/3 cup sugar

2 eggs

3/4 cup self-rising flour

CARAMEL SAUCE

2 cups sugar

1 cup heavy cream

Pinch of salt

PREPARATION

CAKE Preheat oven to 325 degrees.

In a food processor pulse together dates, coffee, baking soda, vanilla, and butter until semi smooth, scraping sides if necessary. Add eggs and sugar and blend well.

Add flour and blend until just incorporated.

Divide batter into 10 sprayed muffin tins and bake for approximately 13 minutes, or until golden brown.

SAUCE While cakes are baking, place a medium heavy sauce pan over high heat until hot.

Gradually add the 2 cups sugar to pan, whisking as necessary until all sugar is melted and amber in color.

Lower heat to medium-low and slowly whisk in cream.
Strain and set aside to cool slightly.

FINISH Drizzle caramel over cakes and bake for an additional minute. Serve with extra caramel sauce and candied pecans.

Makes 10 cakes

Mark Mannin

H & H RESTAURANT

WHEN OUT-OF-TOWN VISITORS COME FOR BREAKFAST OR LUNCH AT MACON'S H&H RESTAURANT, they seldom leave as soon as they've finished their meal, says the well-known eatery's General Manager, Mark Manning.

"They like to soak up the history," Manning said. And so, patrons tend to hang out after dining and browse the many photos on the walls—photos of the Allman Brothers and other music stars who have dined at the restaurant over the years. This dining room is where Mama Louise Hudson and the late Mama Inez Hill often fed the Allman Brothers for free in the early 1970s, when the Allmans were just getting their start.

Visitors these days are delighted to meet Mama Louise and tell her how much they enjoyed their meal, whether it was breakfast or lunch. An H&H breakfast might include fried chicken and fried or poached egg tucked into a fluffy biscuit. Lunch offers such choices as a traditional "meat plus three" with fried chicken, biscuit and a choice of various yummy veggies.

"At the same time, we want to offer a bit more than what's traditionally been done," Manning said, "and we would like to bring in a younger clientele as well, so we're pushing specialties. For example, we now offer waffles—something we think the younger clientele will like—as well as the usual items on the menu."

Manning said that when he was in high school, he sometimes skipped school to come to H&H and eat. He has been dining at H&H since 1985. Now as general manager, he said, he loves seeing people come in and be happy with the food and the fascinating history the restaurant offers.

"H&H serves about 120 diners on a good day," Manning said, "and some people come three or four times a week. We take the best care we can of all of our customers by upholding the traditions of H&H."

MEATLOAF

INGREDIENTS

2 pounds of 80/20 ground beef
1/2 onion, *chopped*
1/4 red bell pepper, *chopped*
3 eggs, *beaten*
Salt and pepper to taste

PREPARATION

Preheat oven to 375 degrees.

In a large mixing bowl, combine beef, vegetables, and beaten eggs with salt and pepper to taste.

Once thoroughly combined, form meatloaf mix into a loaf on a greased baking sheet.

Bake for 15 minutes or until an internal temperature of 160 degrees is reached.

Cut into portions and serve hot.

Serves 4

DEVILED EGGS

INGREDIENTS

4 eggs
1/4 cup mayo
1/4 teaspoon yellow mustard
3/4 teaspoon relish of your choice
1/8 cup white vinegar
Pepper to taste
Paprika for garnish

PREPARATION

In a large sauce pan add water and white vinegar. Bring to a rolling boil. Carefully add the eggs to the water/vinegar mixture and boil for 13 minutes.

After the eggs have cooked, immediately drain eggs and place in an ice bath for 5 minutes minimum to stop the eggs from cooking. Split the cooked eggs in half lengthwise, remove the yolk, and reserve in mixing bowl. Mash the yolk with a fork until no large chunks are left. Add mayo, mustard, relish, and pepper and mix thoroughly. Spoon yolk mixture into the halved egg whites and sprinkle with paprika to garnish.

Serves 4

COLLARD GREENS

INGREDIENTS

2 strips of bacon
2 pounds collard greens
1 large ham hock
1/8 tablespoon pepper
1/2 tablespoon seasoning salt
2 gallons water
1/8 cup white vinegar

PREPARATION

In a large stock pot combine water, white vinegar, bacon strips, and ham hock and bring to a rolling boil.

Add all of the seasonings and chopped collards to the pot. *Note: The collards will wilt and take up less space in the pot. It is usually not necessary to add extra water.*

Bring the pot back to a boil, reduce heat, and simmer until the desired tenderness is reached.

Serves 8 to 10

CORNBREAD

INGREDIENTS

DRY MIX

3 cups AP flour
3 cups corn meal
3 tablespoons baking powder
1/2 cup sugar
1 teaspoon salt

WET MIX

1 1/2 cups milk
1 1/2 cups heavy cream
1 cup melted butter
6 eggs
1 teaspoon salt

PREPARATION

Preheat oven to 350 degrees.

In one mixing bowl, combine all the wet ingredients, and in another bowl, mix all of the dry ingredients.

Add the dry mix to the wet mix and gently blend together.

Do not overmix the cornbread or it will not have the desired texture.

Serves 8 to 12

BREAD PUDDING

INGREDIENTS

2 eggs
1 quart milk
3/4 teaspoon vanilla
1/2 cup honey
1 1/2 cups sugar
10 cups cubed bread
3/4 teaspoon nutmeg
Powdered sugar for garnish

PREPARATION

Preheat oven to 350 degrees. In a large mixing bowl combine and whisk the eggs, sugar, milk, vanilla, and nutmeg until the sugar has dissolved. Once thoroughly mixed, carefully incorporate the bread into the wet mix. *Do not overmix or you will mash the bread*.

Once all is blended together, place in the refrigerator for a minimum of 1 hour but no more than 8 hours.

Place pudding mixture into a heavily greased and/or lined casserole dish of your choice—preferably an 8x9 pan. Bake for 30 minutes and remove from the oven.

Apply the honey to the top of the pudding and spread evenly. Return to the oven for 30 minutes and cook until a knife or cake tester can be cleanly removed. If not served immediately, cool completely in the refrigerator. Cut and garnish with powdered sugar and serve.

Serves 8 to 12

PARISH ON CHERRY

THE FIRST TIME VINCENT KELLY AND CHRISSY EISZNER approached the old vacant building at 580 Cherry Street, they gazed into its large front windows, hoping to find a home inside for a dream they shared.

They knew that the building once housed a bar and also had been a hotel. They knew the building was vacant. What they didn't know was whether it suited their dream.

"We looked into the windows," Vincent said, "and I told Chrissy, 'This is it!'"

Today, the building's main floor houses Parish on Cherry, a popular and thriving upscale New Orleans-style eatery and bar. The place is so much like New Orleans that you think you're actually in New Orleans until you walk outside and discover that you're still in Macon.

Chrissy and Vincent met in 2004 when both were working in a Chili's restaurant in Florida. Both had visited New Orleans frequently and loved the old city. As they became friends, they realized that they shared a desire to open a New Orleans Cajun style restaurant somewhere. Chrissy, whose home was in Macon, was familiar with this area, so they began searching here and found what has turned out to be just the right place.

First, there was quite a bit of necessary clean-up and remodeling of the old building's main floor. Plumbing and electrical upgrades were installed. Two rooms behind what is now the restaurant were torn out and replaced by a walk-in cooler. The ceiling and walls were painted in New Orleans colors: purple ceiling, green walls, also some gold.

"Everything was trial and error," Vincent said. "We worked on it for a year before we opened, even snagged people in from the sidewalk to admire what we were doing. Macon really embraced us."

People began bringing unexpected gifts: souvenirs from New Orleans, horse shoes for good luck, decorations such as fleur de lis for the restaurant's walls. The walls also have some of the early 1900s hotel's original window shutters.

"We were delighted," Chrissy said. "We wanted people to put their footprint onto it, and they did."

What's more, the cooks and servers, ages around 30 to 40, have become a close and compatible group, and some now are managers.

Parish on Cherry is open Sundays through Saturdays for lunch and supper, and there is live music nightly.

Chrissy Eiszner and Vincent Kelly

ÉTOUFFÉE

INGREDIENTS

1/4 cup unsalted butter
1/4 cup flour
1 cup water
1 cup onion, *diced*
1/2 cup celery, *diced*
1/2 cup bell pepper, *diced*
2 tablespoons garlic, *chopped*
1 teaspoon thyme
1 cup tomatoes, *diced*
1 tablespoon Cajun seasoning
1 teaspoon Old Bay
1 tablespoon Worcestershire
1/4 tablespoon hot sauce
1/4 teaspoon black pepper
1/4 teaspoon salt
1/2 cup parsley, chopped
6 jumbo shrimp *(16/20) peeled and deveined*
Cooked white rice

PREPARATION

Melt butter in large pot over medium heat, stir until it starts to brown, sprinkle in flour while continually mixing and simmer until it turns a dark brown color—about 10-15 minutes.

Add onions, celery, and pepper to the roux and cook until vegetables are tender—about 10-12 minutes.

Add garlic, thyme, and parsley and cook for 1 minute.

Whisk in water, add tomatoes, Cajun seasoning, Old Bay, salt, pepper, Worcestershire sauce and simmer for about 25-30 minutes.

In a separate pan, melt garlic butter over medium-high heat.

Add 6 shrimp to skillet and season with salt and pepper to taste. Cook for 2 minutes or until shrimp becomes pink in color, flip shrimp once and cook for 1 minute or until cooked thoroughly.

Serve over white rice, top with 6 grilled shrimp. Garnish with parsley and a sprinkle of Old Bay.

Serves 1

CHARGRILLED OYSTERS

Serves 2 to 6

INGREDIENTS

12 fresh oysters, *un-shucked*
Handful fresh parsley, *chopped*
2 cups panko breadcrumbs
1/4 cup butter, *melted*
1 teaspoon Cajun seasoning
1/4 cup parmesan cheese, *grated*
1 teaspoon white pepper
1 tablespoon fresh garlic, *minced*

PREPARATION

Shuck oysters and discard the top shell. Rinse oysters under cold running water to remove any sand or debris.

In a separate bowl, mix all other ingredients until thoroughly mixed.

Place 1 tablespoon of mixture on top of oyster. Place oyster over an open flame on grill. Cook until the butter begins to boil and the edge of the shell will become black.

BANANAS FOSTER

Serves 1 to 2

INGREDIENTS

1 banana, *cut in half lengthwise*
2 tablespoons butter
1/4 cup light brown sugar
4 ounces butterscotch schnapps
2 scoops vanilla ice cream
Cinnamon and sugar to taste

PREPARATION

Heat brown sugar and butter in a pan over medium heat until melted.

Add butterscotch schnapps and banana to mixture and cook for 1 minute or until the sauce caramelizes.

Pour mixture over ice cream.

Sprinkle cinnamon and sugar over top.

THE PERFECT PEAR

WHEN MEGAN WILSON-BRENT WAS A CHILD, she loved to play restaurant. Later, a family friend gave her some cooking lessons, but it wasn't until much later that she appreciated her own culinary skills.

"I liked it," she said. "I was good at it, good at numbers and quantities, and I loved the cooking and the visiting."

Megan opened her first restaurant on Carroll Street in downtown Perry. It was so well received that it gradually became too small to accommodate its growing numbers of hungry customers. So, after three years, she moved up Carroll Street into the larger space that the restaurant occupies today. She named her new digs The Perfect Pear.

The name is the result of a gift Megan once received, a pear-shaped paperweight with a sparkling sugar-like coating. "The name Perfect Pear came to me from the gift," she said. "And, so, we have The Perfect Pear Catering."

Its dining room is elegant, with snow white walls and dark red appointments. The tables are set with crisp white cloths and small centerpieces of colorful blossoms in glass vases. The room seats 75, and outside of regular hours is available for private parties such as club meetings, wedding parties and family functions.

"We've been on Carroll Street eight years now, and we've seen a lot of changes" Megan said. "There's great support here for small businesses and much camaraderie."

The restaurant purchases many products from area farmers. "We're big on buying local and supporting our local farmers and businesses," she said.

On a menu that features a wealth of yummy items, The Perfect Pear's dining room boasts two year-round favorites: a tomato bisque and a delicious pimento cheese that's served in a burger or as a bacon and cheese sandwich. The bisque is served piping hot, but no one minds. "Even if the weather is 110 degrees in July, we're still going to be selling those two items," Megan said.

Although she loves every aspect of her job, she concedes that it isn't an easy one.

"You have to have a love for this," she said, smiling. "I'm the chef, I'm the owner, I'm the dishwasher, and I do payroll. You've got to love it, just got to love it, if you're going to do it."

Megan has worked in restaurants for 20-plus years with some amazing chefs and owners. Perry, she said, has "been wonderful to us."

Megan Wilson-Brent

BUTTER

PERFECT BLACKBERRY COBBLER

INGREDIENTS

2 cups fresh blackberries
1 1/2 cups sugar
6 tablespoons butter
1 cup self-rising flour
1 cup heavy whipping cream

PREPARATION

Pre-heat oven to 350 degrees.

Melt butter, in oven, in a 9x13 baking dish.

In a metal bowl whisk flour, whipping cream and one cup of sugar. The mixture will be thick. Use a rubber spatula or spoon to transfer mixture to baking dish with melted butter. *No need to stir, or fret if the butter and batter mix.*

Toss washed, whole blackberries in remaining 1/2 cup of sugar and spoon over batter. Bake for 30-45 minutes until golden brown.

Pairs, perfectly, with vanilla ice cream!

Serves 24

BLACKENED AHI TUNA
PEACH SALSA, ZUCCHINI AND SQUASH NOODLES

Serves 6

INGREDIENTS

6, 4- or 6-ounce ahi tuna steaks
5-6 ripe Georgia peaches, *diced*
2 tablespoons fresh lime juice
Salt and pepper to taste
3 large zucchini
4 tablespoons olive oil
2 teaspoons red onion, *chopped*
1 large garlic clove, *pressed*
3 large yellow squash
2 tablespoons fresh cilantro, *chopped*
Paul Prudhomme's Blackened Redfish Magic

PREPARATION

Generously coat tuna steaks with blackening seasoning. In a glass or stainless bowl combine peaches, red onion, lime juice, garlic and cilantro. Gently toss with a spoon or your hands to avoid bruising the peaches. Season with salt and pepper. Refrigerate salsa mixture until ready to serve. Using a julienne tool, slice zucchini and squash into thin ribbons.

Sauté ribbons in 2 teaspoons of olive oil until desired tenderness.

Heat olive oil in large heavy skillet or griddle pan over medium-high heat. The oil should dance a little, but not smoke. Sear seasoned tuna steaks for approximately 3 minutes on each side. Place each tuna steak atop vegetable ribbons and top with peach salsa.

BRUISED PURPLE POTATO SALAD

Serves 10 to 12

INGREDIENTS

3 pounds small purple potatoes
1/4 cup blue cheese crumbles
3 green onions, *chopped*
Salt and pepper to taste
1/4 cup white balsamic vinegar
1/4 cup extra virgin olive oil
1 small garlic clove, *pressed*
Dash salt and pepper
1/2 teaspoon Dijon mustard

PREPARATION

While bringing four quarts of salted water to a boil; whisk together white balsamic vinegar, olive oil, pressed garlic, Dijon mustard, salt, and pepper. Refrigerate until needed.

Place halved potatoes in boiling water and cook until fork tender.

Toss the drained potatoes, blue cheese and green onion in a bowl. Drizzle with white balsamic vinaigrette. Serve warm or cold.

Bruce Loc Nguye

PHO SAIGON

WHEN TRYING TO THINK OF RESTAURANTS TO INVITE TO PARTICIPATE IN THE COOKBOOK, Pho Saigon Noodle House in Macon was at the top of the list. On their Facebook page, one customer writes, "Everything we ordered was delicious."

Pho, pronounced "FUH," is a Vietnamese noodle soup consisting of broth, linguine-shaped rice noodles, a few specific herbs, and meat. Pho restaurants have become somewhat of a hip trend in large cities over the last two decades so it comes as a little surprise that Macon has such a gem. The noodle bowls are large and are served with as many as twelve garnishes, such as a variety of onions, basil, Thai chili peppers, lemon and lime wedges, bean sprouts, cilantro, fish sauce, hoisin, and hot chili sauce. Like any traditional Vietnamese noodle house, Pho Saigon offers a variety of Pho bowls and customers can even design their own bowl.

Pho Saigon, owned and operated by Bruce and his wife, offers a family style atmosphere where their children are often heard playing while their parents are busy cooking and serving customers. A true mom and pop operation, Bruce and his wife are welcoming, warm and exceptional hosts in dishing out authentic and fresh Vietnamese cuisine.

Like many Asian restaurants, the menu is large with an easy numbering system for ordering. Other popular dishes at Pho Saigon are the Bahn Mi sandwiches, crafted on Vietnamese bread that is made fresh daily, along with their fresh spring rolls and fried egg rolls. Bruce says he loves such recipes as the spring roll and the Vietnamese crispy noodle because they're "extremely versatile in that you can fill them with almost any meat and veggie you want." This is important to his philosophy regarding food, "cook what you like to eat and it will always be satisfying!"

So whether you love quail eggs and squid or like to play it safe, many of the dishes at Pho Saigon may cater to your specific taste. Each dish, more colorful than the last, is made with only the freshest ingredients, and can be washed down with Vietnamese Iced Coffee or Bubble Tea. The smells alone are sure to have your mouth watering before you even get a chance to say "Pho, please."

PHO BO
VIETNAMESE BEEF NOODLE SOUP

INGREDIENTS

10 ounces dried rice noodles
40 ounces beef broth
8 ounces eye round steak *sliced very thin*
Fresh ginger root
1 teaspoon salt
2 teaspoons sugar
1 teaspoon cilantro seed
1 teaspoon cinnamon
1 teaspoon star anise
White onion, *thinly sliced*
Green onion, *for garnish*
Handful of fresh cilantro
Fresh basil leaves, *for garnish*
Bean sprouts, *for garnish*
Lime or lemon juice
Jalapeño, *sliced for garnish*
1 tablespoon hoisin sauce
1 tablespoon sriracha hot sauce
Black pepper

PREPARATION

Pour the beef broth into the sauce pan, then add white onion, salt, sugar, fresh ginger, cilantro seed, cinnamon, and star anise. Bring to a boil and then simmer for 15 minutes.

In a separate bowl, boil the rice noodles for approximately 2 minutes.

Rinse noodles and set in large serving bowl.

Top the noodles with the steak, leftover white onion, green onion, and cilantro.

Pour the very hot broth into the bowl. Add black pepper, fresh basil, beansprout, more cilantro, lime juice, and jalapeño.

Serve with hoisin sauce and sriracha hot sauce to add extra flavor.

Serves 1

VIETNAMESE SPRING ROLLS
WITH PEANUT SAUCE

SPRING ROLLS

1 package of rice paper wrappers
1/2 pound raw shrimp; peeled and deveined
1 bunch fresh mint or cilantro leaves
1 head of green leaf lettuce
1 bunch bean sprouts
1 package of rice vermicelli noodles; cooked

Cook the shrimp in hot water and cut in half, down the middle. Wet the rice paper and wait for it to soften before adding the ingredients and rolling. Put the shrimp down on the rice paper first, pink side facing out. Continue to fill with additional ingredients using caution as to not over fill, otherwise you will not be able to close the roll. Serve with peanut sauce.

Serves 2

PEANUT SAUCE

1 cup water
8 tablespoons creamy peanut butter
8 tablespoons hoisin sauce
4 tablespoons granulated sugar

Mix all ingredients together in small pot over medium-low heat until the sugar is dissolved and the sauce is well combined.

CRISPY NOODLES
VIETNAMESE STYLE

INGREDIENTS

1 bunch fresh egg noodle
Vegetable oil
10 fresh prawns, *peeled and deveined*
5 fresh small squid, *cleaned and sliced small*
5 fresh scallops, *cleaned and cut in half*
3 teaspoons garlic, *minced*
1 onion, *sliced*
Mushrooms, *sliced*
Chinese cabbage, *sliced*
Bok choy, *sliced*
Broccoli, *sliced*
Carrot, *peeled and sliced*
8 ounces chicken broth
1/2 teaspoon soy sauce
1/2 teaspoon oyster sauce
1/2 teaspoon sesame oil
1/2 teaspoon sugar
Pinch pepper
Pinch salt
1 teaspoon tapioca starch
Green onion and cilantro

PREPARATION

Heat enough oil to cover all the noodles and fry until they are crispy and turn a brownish-yellow. Drain on paper towels. In same oil and pan, add garlic and fry until fragrant.

Add all seafood and stir fry quickly for 2-3 minutes. Add sliced onion, Chinese cabbage, bok choy, carrots, green broccoli and stir fry 4-5 minutes. Season with salt, pepper, chicken broth, soy sauce, oyster sauce, fish sauce, sesame oil, and sugar.

Pour a big spoonful of water into pan, add a little tapioca starch and toss until thick sauce forms. Pour the sauce, seafood and vegetables over the deep fried egg noodle and garnish with fresh cilantro and green onion. Serve hot. *Substitute seafood, protein, or vegetables to liking.*

Serves 1

Brandon Pippin and Pietro Bongiovan

PIETRO'S

EXPECTATIONS WERE HIGH FOR PIETRO'S. Pietro Bongiovanni worked at Natalia's for ten years, five of those as the Executive Chef. Many know Natalia's as one of the elite in Central Georgia's list of dining establishments. However, Pietro stated that it was time to be independently creative and looked forward to making his own schedule, which led him to open his own Italian restaurant located off of Bass Road in Macon.

Pietro's officially opened in April of 2016 on the corner of a small strip of businesses. The building had housed a restaurant before but there were still changes to be made to really make it feel like his project. He and his team refurbished the bar and built tall, wooden walls that separate the larger back booths from one another. The inside has a cement floor and touches of rock offering a rustic, relaxed setting. The kitchen is open, creating a relationship between diner and cook. One issue they ran into was waiting on their liquor license. Pietro decided they would go ahead and open.They allowed customers to bring in their own alcohol in the meantime, which he says customers loved.

Pietro's father, a former restaurant owner himself, moved from Italy to Germany where he met Pietro's mother. Pietro was born in Germany and played tennis growing up where he excelled and received a scholarship to come to the states to play and go to school. However, he needed a job while in school so he was hired as a cook and in his words, "got stuck in the business." Thankfully he did because his food is amazing. His menu offers simple Italian dishes, using fresh ingredients. Something as basic as a penne pasta with cream sauce is taken to a new level as the pasta is made in house and ingredients are sourced locally. The shrimp, some of the largest you've ever seen and sautéed to perfection, have become one of the many food items that customers rave about. Pietro says typically they try to offer up to five specials on top of the usual dinner menu, including at least one appetizer, fish, filet and pasta dish. Additionally, menu items are modified by seasonal ingredients.

Everything from vegetables to proteins are purchased from local sources such as White Oak Farms and Rocking Chair Ranch.

"The biggest challenge has been to locally source all of our ingredients. Many people turn away from doing it because it comes with a hefty price tag or can be difficult to get food items you need." Pietro hopes to educate people on the importance of eating more organic, wholesome food and it has become something he and his team stand for.

GEORGIA COAST SHRIMP SCAMPI

Serves 4

INGREDIENTS

1 pound Georgia shrimp, *deveined in shell*

1 teaspoon parsley, *chopped*

1 teaspoon fresh oregano, *chopped*

2 teaspoons garlic

1/4 cup white wine

2 lemons, *juiced*

Zest of 1 lemon

Salt and pepper to taste

PREPARATION

In a large sauté pan, add olive oil. Add shrimp and cook until three-fourths done.

Add the wine and all other ingredients. Cook until the wine reduces by half. Serve with crusty bread.

JUMBO KING SCALLOPS

INGREDIENTS

1 pound scallops
1/4 teaspoon salt
1 cup pumpernickel bread crumbs
1/4 teaspoon pepper

TARRAGON AIOLI

1 teaspoon garlic, *minced*
1 cup mayonnaise
1/4 cup Dijon mustard
1/4 cup fresh tarragon, *chopped*

PICKLED CABBAGE

1/2 head red cabbage, *julienne*
1 cup granulated sugar
1 cup sherry vinegar
Salt and pepper to taste

PREPARATION

AIOLI Combine cabbage, sherry vinegar, sugar, salt, and pepper and cook on low for one hour.

CABBAGE Combine mayo, tarragon, garlic, and mustard and mix well. Refrigerate until needed.

Prepare bread crumbs by combining all ingredients and rinsing scallops. Toss scallops in bread crumbs and sauté on medium/high heat until golden brown on each side.

Spread aioli on plate and top with scallops and pickled cabbage.

Serves 5

SPAGHETTI CARBONARA

Serves 4

INGREDIENTS

1 pound spaghetti noodles

1 pint heavy cream

1/4 pound pancetta

1/2 teaspoon black pepper

1/2 teaspoon fresh garlic, *minced*

1/2 cup parmesan, *grated*

1 tablespoon fresh parsley, *chopped*

4 egg yolks

PREPARATION

Cook spaghetti noodles until *al dente*. In a sauce pan add pancetta and cook until crispy. Add garlic and cream and reduce by three-quarters.

Reduce heat and add the pepper, parsley, and parmesan and stir until the cheese is melted. Turn the heat off and mix in egg yolks. *Be careful as to not curdle the eggs.*

Serve immediately.

CHOCOLATE LAVA CAKE

INGREDIENTS

10 ounces milk chocolate morsels
2 ounces butter
7 eggs, *separated*
1/2 cup granulated sugar
1/2 teaspoon iodized salt

PREPARATION

Preheat the oven to 500 degrees.

Whisk the egg whites in mixing bowl until firm peaks begin to form. Melt chocolate and butter in a double broiler. Whisk in egg yolks, sugar, and salt.

Once all ingredients are incorporated, fold the egg whites into the chocolate and mixture and place into 4-ounce, buttered ramekins. Bake until risen and firm about 6 minutes.

Garnish with whipped cream and serve.

Serves 12

Heinz Krassnig and Maria Runggaldie

RISTORANTE DA MARIA

OUTSIDE OF DUBLIN, ON A 30-ACRE FARM, Ristorante da Maria has brought a delightful touch of Italy to Laurens County. Some of the restaurant's diners have discovered that there's also a place of overnight rest and relaxation in the restaurant's adjacent bed and breakfast.

The owners have named the entire property The Dublin Farm, and they welcome those in search of a truly Italian meal, a class in Italian cooking, or just an overnight stay in a peaceful environment.

Maria Runggaldier and Heinz Krassnig, are the owners of this serene retreat. Maria, who is Italian, is in charge of the kitchen, works with preparation helpers, and does the cooking; Heinz, from Austria, welcomes visitors to the dining room, suggests tasty menu items, pours the wine, and takes the plates.

"I am the front man," he said with a grin.

Heinz explained how he and Maria met: He had a job hiring and firing people for a company in Bolzano, a small town in the northern part of Italy. Maria came for a job interview. "So, then we both had a job for life," he said with a big smile.

The couple knew that they wanted to come to the United States to open a B&B and one that offered Italian fine dining. They visited three times in search of the perfect place and made the final decision to put down roots in Dublin.

As a Dublin resident said later, "Dublin won!"

The restaurant has been a huge success, and from time to time, groups attend Maria's cooking classes. She works all day to prepare, choosing a five-course Italian menu. The class takes about three hours, then they eat for another two hours. "It's especially fun when the people know each other," Heinz said.

Sometimes an entire office staff will come for a cooking class. The local Health Department did, for example. And Maria has given a cooking class at Robins Air Force Base.

Heinz noted that all of Ristorante's food is fresh, coming from local farms. "And when people see it is all fresh, they come back again," he said.

The couple has also opened a coffee shop, now owned and operated by Heinz's daughter, Nora, and her husband, Juan, in Dublin. My CoffeeShop is a small, artisan coffee shop in the heart of Dublin's downtown.

Be sure to head to Dublin and check out a cooking class with friends, catch some Zzz's at the B&B or just simply enjoy some of Maria's fresh Italian cuisine. Heinz and Maria are a perfect pair of hosts and the scenery alone is enough to make you want to return again and again.

BOLOGNESE MEAT SAUCE

INGREDIENTS

2 tablespoons butter
4 tablespoons olive oil
1 medium onion, *finely chopped*
2 tablespoons pancetta or bacon *finely chopped*
1 carrot, *finely chopped*
1 stalk celery, *finely chopped*
1 clove garlic, *finely chopped*
12 ounces lean ground beef
Salt and pepper
1/2 cup dry white wine
3/4 cup beef or chicken stock
14-ounce can of plum tomatoes *chopped with juice*
1 bay leaf
1/4 tablespoon fresh nutmeg *grated*

PREPARATION

Heat the butter and oil in a heavy saucepan, add the onion and cook over moderate heat for 3-4 minutes.

Add the pancetta and cook until the onion is translucent. Stir in the carrot, celery, and garlic. Cook 3-4 minutes more.

Add the beef and crumble it into the vegetables with a fork. Stir until the meat loses its red color. Season with salt and pepper.

Pour in the wine and raise the heat slightly until the liquid evaporates (about 3-4 minutes).

Add the beef or chicken stock and cook. Stir in the tomatoes with their juice and the herbs. Bring the sauce to a boil.

Reduce the heat to low and simmer, uncovered for 1.5 to 2 hours, stirring occasionally. Add more salt and pepper to taste.

This sauce is a perfect topping for your favorite pasta and can also be used with baked lasagna. Vist RebuildingMacon.org for the lasagna and other recipes.

Makes 8 to 10 servings

STRAWBERRY TIRAMISU

INGREDIENTS

1 pound strawberries
washed and hulled

7 ounces lady fingers

1 teaspoon cornstarch

6 ounces granulated sugar

2 cups heavy whipping cream

1 teaspoon vanilla extract

8 ounces mascarpone
or cream cheese

5 ounces yogurt, *plain*

4-5 ounces powdered sugar

1 tablespoon chopped pistachios

PREPARATION

Place the strawberries in a sauce pan and purée until smooth. Stir in the sugar and bring to a simmer.

Add the cornstarch (mixed with 2 tablespoon of water) and whisk constantly until a thick sauce forms.

Line the bottom of a baking dish with lady finger cookies. Spread one half of the hot strawberry sauce over the cookies.

Whip the heavy cream with the vanilla extract in a bowl until stiff peaks are reached.

In a bowl combine the mascarpone with the yogurt and powdered sugar and stir until smooth. Fold in the whipped cream.

Spread one half of the mixture over the cookies. Place the remaining lady fingers on the mascarpone/cream mixture and repeat until you have no more ingredients.

Cover and refrigerate for 5 hours.

Sprinkle with the chopped pistachios and serve garnished with cut strawberries and powdered sugar.

Makes 8 to 10 servings

SALTIMBOCCA
OF VEAL OR CHICKEN

INGREDIENTS

8 veal top round scaloppini or chicken breast

8 slices prosciutto cotto or prosciutto Parma

8 fresh sage leaves

All-purpose flour

Salt and pepper to taste

4 ounces unsalted butter

3/4 cup Marsala wine or dry sherry

PREPARATION

Flatten the slices with a smooth meat mallet, pounding from the center outwards.

Place a thin slice of prosciutto onto each slice of veal and/or chicken.

Place a fresh sage leaf on top of prosciutto and secure with toothpicks.

Lightly coat the veal or chicken slices with flour mixed with salt and pepper.

Melt half of the butter in a skillet and when bubbling, brown the veal or chicken well for about 1 to 2 minutes.

Turn and cook for 1 to 2 minutes more or until brown and cooked through. Transfer veal or chicken to a warm plate.

Add the Marsala wine to the pan and bring to a simmer to reduce the wine a bit. Using a wooden spoon, scrape up any bits from the pan.

Add the second half of the butter to the pan and one tablespoon of flour, whisking constantly until sauce is thickened.

Season to taste with salt and pepper, spoon the sauce over the saltimbocca and serve.

Serves 4

Michael Dean

THE ROOKERY

MICHAEL DEAN HAS BEEN IN THE RESTAURANT BUSINESS FOR 14 YEARS, and has managed The Rookery's well-known restaurant and bar for three-and-a-half of those years.

"I love it!" Dean declares with happy enthusiasm, gazing around at the crowd that's there for lunch on a sunny Saturday.

It's a high noon in June, and The Rook, as it's often called, is filled to capacity with lunchtime diners. Staffers are hurrying to clean one or two tables vacated just moments ago, and a dozen or more hungry people are clustered outside the front door, each hoping the next table will be theirs.

The Rookery is a well-known and popular lunch spot, but it's especially busy on a summer Saturday when whole families—dad, mom and, very often, kids of many ages—come in for a midday meal in either the dining room or on the front patio. The food list is bountiful, and the milkshakes and craft beers are famous for their tastiness. And if you live in Macon, you're highly likely to see people you know there.

"The fun part about The Rookery is that it's very diverse," Dean says. "On most any day it can be business people, law enforcement, a courthouse crowd, families with kids—there's a very large mix of people who show up."

Over the years, visiting celebrities also have learned the way to The Rookery. Film stars who have been spotted at The Rook include Jeff Foxworthy and Kiefer Sutherland. Frank Azari, who voices for TV's "The Simpsons," also has dined there, and singer Jason Isbel, too.

"And this is Greg Allman's favorite spot when he comes to town," says Dean.

Macon businessmen Wes Griffith and Chad Evans, founders of The Moonhanger Group, spotted the potential for upgrading The Rookery and other downtown Macon spots in a time when many businesses were closing or moving to outlying areas. Moonhanger Group also operates other downtown businesses including H&H Restaurant, made famous by the Allman Brothers, the Cox Capitol Theatre, and also has opened the popular Dovetail restaurant upstairs over The Rookery as well as their latest venture, El Camino Taqueria and Cantina.

The Rookery is a busy place almost anytime you go there, whether you're in for lunch, or supper, or just to meet friends for a drink and conversation. It may be a fact that unless you have eaten at The Rookery, you haven't experienced Macon. Next time you're there, order the Jimmy Carter burger topped with peanut butter and bacon, it's surprisingly popular and sure to be a burger to remember.

THE ROOKERY BURGER

INGREDIENTS

2, 4-ounce burger patties, *thin*
2 slices American cheese
2 ounces yellow onions, *diced*
Dill pickle chips
1 ounce Coca Cola ketchup
1 ounce mustard
Bakery Roll

PREPARATION

Cook two seasoned burger patties on a flat griddle.

Sauté onions in a skillet.

Top both patties with American cheese and stack on top of each other.

Top stacked burger patties with sautéed onions, dill pickle chips, ketchup, and mustard.

Serve on a toasted bakery roll with lettuce, tomatoes, and red onion.

Serves 1

KING BEE WRAP

Serves 1

INGREDIENTS

Three chicken tenders, *chopped*

1, 12-inch tortilla wrap

2 ounces cheese, *shredded*

1 ounce Crystal hot sauce

2 ounces honey mustard

2 ounces pimento cheese

PREPARATION

Warm tortilla on a griddle.

Combine all other ingredients in a bowl and mix.

Place ingredients on warm wrap and roll into a burrito, folding in at the ends.

Slice on a bias and serve.

STANKONIA FRIED CHICKEN SANDWICH

Serves 1

INGREDIENTS

1, 6-ounce fried chicken breast
4 ounces Mrs. Griffin's hot BBQ sauce
2 ounces collard greens
2 ounces prosciutto
1 slice Swiss cheese
Bakery roll

PREPARATION

Sauté collards and prosciutto in a pan until hot.

Toss fried chicken in Mrs. Griffin's hot sauce.

Toast bakery roll with butter on a griddle.

Place chicken on bottom bun and top with Swiss cheese.

Top with collard and prosciutto mixture. *Great with pepper sauce!*

Kim Sheridan and General Manager, Calvin Clark

THE SWANSON

IT'S LUNCHTIME ON A WEEKDAY IN DOWNTOWN PERRY and it's likely that every table at The Swanson, both indoors and on the porch, is filled.

Many of the diners are local residents and business people, but The Swanson, known for its fascinating history, charming decor and delicious Southern style food, draws customers from miles around.

Dating from the 1880s, the lovely house began as three rooms and, gradually, was enlarged as it changed owners. It was the home of a former Perry mayor named Cox, then was purchased in 1903 by Nora Singleton Cox, grandmother of Ms. Norine Swanson-Jones, for whom the house now is named.

It was Ms. Swanson-Jones who opened Perry's first kindergarten in the house in the 1930s, a kindergarten that has sparked a fascinating belief that the house is haunted by the spirits of the children.

"We are haunted," said Kim Sheridan, who owns the restaurant today with her husband, Mike. After hearing voices of children at play, finding children's fingerprints on mirrors, and once finding water left running overnight in a bathroom, the Sheridans brought in ghost hunters, who spent the night in the house and also heard children playing.

"They heard the children's voices, and said they were voices of friendly spirits," Mrs. Sheridan said.

The Sheridans purchased the house in 2002, and in the beginning they did all the cooking themselves. Now they rely on 30 employees, five or six of them in the kitchen at any one time, and each one specializing in a food—collards, squash, rutabagas, etc.

Mike and Kim often preach the importance of sitting and taking time to enjoy one's company while dining at their Southern, antebellum style restaurant. The house has hosted many wedding rehearsal dinners and they've catered off-site functions, "But we really like to stick with what we know best," Kim said, "everyday home cooking."

CHERRIED CHICKEN

Serves 4

INGREDIENTS

4, 6-ounce chicken breasts
boneless, skinless

1 can dark sweet cherries

1/4 cup orange juice

1 cup brown sugar

2 tablespoons cornstarch

1 teaspoon dry mustard

PREPARATION

Preheat oven to 350 degrees. Salt and pepper chicken and place in full-size pan. Bake for approximately 20 minutes.

Mix other ingredients and cook over low heat in 2 quart sauce pan until thickened.

Remove chicken from oven. Pour mixture over cooked chicken and return to oven and continue baking for 30 minutes or until tender.

COPPER PENNIES

INGREDIENTS

2 pounds fresh carrots, *sliced*
1 large onion, *diced*
1 green bell pepper, *diced*
1 can tomato soup
1/2 cup salad oil
1 cup sugar
3/4 cup apple cider vinegar
1 teaspoon mustard
1 teaspoon Worcestershire sauce
1/4 teaspoon salt
1/4 teaspoon pepper

PREPARATION

Slice carrots crossways in a round shape (to resemble pennies).

Add onions and bell peppers to carrots in bowl.

Combine all other ingredients and pour over vegetables, mix and toss well. Refrigerate for 2 days.

Serve chilled.

Serves 12

BREAD PUDDING
WITH CARAMEL SAUCE

INGREDIENTS

PUDDING

1/2 loaf white sandwich bread *diced*

3 eggs

3/4cups granulated sugar

1/4 teaspoon salt

2 tablespoons vanilla extract

1/2 teaspoon cinnamon

1 1/4 cups half and half, *scalded*

SAUCE

1/2 pound margarine

3/4 pound light brown sugar

3/4 cup light corn syrup

1/2 cup heavy cream

PREPARATION

PUDDING Preheat oven to 300 degrees.

Put diced bread in greased 9x13 full pan.

Beat eggs. Add in sugar, salt, cinnamon, vanilla, and half and half.

Pour over bread. Press bread into mixture.

Allow pan to set at least 15 minutes. Press bread into mixture again.

Cover with inverted lid and bake for 1.5 hours.

Pudding is done when it "jiggles" as a whole unit.

SAUCE Combine light brown sugar, margarine, and corn syrup in sauce pan.

Heat over medium heat, stirring constantly until sugar is dissolved.

Remove from heat and stir in heavy cream.

Serves 12

Matthew Hammock

TIC TOC ROOM

MATTHEW HAMMOCK BEGAN working in Macon's Tic Toc Room not quite two years ago. Hammock, who received much of his training in downtown Savannah restaurants, found himself more or less in charge of the Tic Toc Room kitchen, and he began making some gradual changes. One of those changes is an increased number of available seafood dishes.

"Tic Toc usually had seafood once a week," Chef Hammock said. "Now we order it two to three times a week."

Having recently been named executive chef by Tic Toc Owner Cesare Mammarella, Chef Hammock has made additional changes as well. "Sushi is coming off the menu," he said. "It's been on it for years. We'll have more small plates, appetizers, and Southern things like marinated artichokes grilled with hollandaise. My philosophy is to keep things simple, with minimal ingredients, but keep them fresh."

Born and raised in Macon, Chef Hammock attended Tattnall Square Academy before attending the Culinary Institute of Savannah and landing his first real job, solo chef at Savannah's Flip Flop Tiki Bar and Grill. On returning to Macon a couple of years ago, he was hired by Mammarella who named him executive chef when the position came open.

"Matthew has done very well, bringing in new flavors and starting things back much like they first were," Mammarella said. "He shows an incredible amount of maturity, and takes criticism very well in this ego-driven business. I can see him as an owner."

New marketing and beverage directors also have been added recently to Tic Toc's staff of just over a dozen workers, and the Tic Toc has recently hosted a couple of wine dinners, one touching on California wines, the other called Barcelona Nights.

"The beverage director wants to see four to five wine dinners a year," Mammarella said, "and we're getting back to wine pairings with foods."

He added that some interior remodeling also is in the plans for the building.

"A remodel is coming near the end of the year," he said. "I want to open up the look and feel of the kitchen, having it more involved with the diners. We're thinking of removing a wall and having some kind of visible station."

A private dining room upstairs is also in the plans to be remodeled.

OSTRICH MEDALLIONS

INGREDIENTS

3, 2-ounce ostrich medallions
3 sprigs thyme
2 garlic cloves, crushed
1 ounce cold butter
1/2 cup cream
1 tablespoon salt and pepper
1 tablespoon olive oil

PREPARATION

In a sauce pan add olive oil and heat on high.

Lightly dust ostrich in salt and pepper and place in hot oil to sear.

Add garlic and thyme and cold butter.

Roast until you smell the aromas of the thyme.

Add the cream and boil until bubbles are dime sized.

Serve with your favorite style mashed potatoes and vegetables.

Serves 1

SILVER OAK CELLAR

LOBSTER RAVIOLI
WITH SHRIMP

Serves 1

INGREDIENTS

1 tablespoon olive oil

1/3 cup roma tomatoes, *chopped*

1 tablespoon basil, *chiffonade*

6 jumbo shrimp

1/2 cup cream

1/4 cup white wine

1 tablespoon asiago cheese, *grated*

Box favorite ravioli pasta

PREPARATION

In a sauce pan, add olive oil under high heat. Once pan is hot, add tomatoes, basil, and shrimp.

Deglaze with white wine and then add the cream. Boil until the bubbles become dime sized. Fold in the asiago cheese.

Lower heat and begin boiling ravioli in separate sauce pot. Transfer ravioli to sauce pan and stir. Garnish with more basil and asiago cheese.

TUNA TARTARE

INGREDIENTS

3 ounces tuna filet, *diced*

1 teaspoon cucumber, *brunoise*

1 teaspoon green onion, *chopped*

1 teaspoon lemon oil

Salt and pepper to taste

1 tablespoon sweet wasabi whipped cream

1 tablespoon citrus soy reduction

4 crispy wonton chips

3 avocado slices, *thin*

PREPARATION

In a small mixing bowl mix tuna, cucumber, onion, and lemon oil with a pinch of salt and pepper.

Top with avocado slices and serve with wonton chips, wasabi whip, and citrus soy reduction.

Serves 1

RESTAURANT GUIDE

1842 INN
353 College Street
Macon, GA 31201
478-741-1842
1842Inn.com

AUBRI LANE'S
114 South Wayne Street
Milledgeville, GA 31061
478-454-4181
AubriLanes.com

THE BACK BURNER
2242 Ingleside Avenue
Macon, GA 31204
478-746-3336
BackBurnerMacon.com

BEARFOOT TAVERN
468 Second Street
Macon, GA 31201
478-305-7703
HotPlatesGroup.com

BRASSERIE CIRCA
4420 Forsyth Road
Macon, GA 31210
478-621-4140
HotPlatesGroup.com

BURKE MANSION
1085 Georgia Avenue
Macon, GA 31201
478-238-1731
BurkeMansionMacon.com

EDGAR'S BISTRO
5171 Eisenhower Parkway
Macon, Ga 31206
478-471-4250
Helms.edu

EL CAMINO
378 Second Street
Macon, Ga 31201
478-257-6393
ElCaminoMacon.com

FOUNTAIN OF JUICE
4123 Forsyth Road
Macon, GA 31210
478-755-5000
FountainOfJuice.it

GREY GOOSE PLAYER'S CLUB
4524 Forsyth Road
Macon, GA 31210
478-471-0987
GreyGoosePlayersClub.com

RESTAURANT GUIDE

GRITS CAFE
17 West Johnston Street
Forsyth, GA 31029
478-994-8325
GritsCafe.com

H&H RESTAURANT
807 Forsyth Street
Macon, GA 31201
478-621-7044

PARISH ON CHERRY
580 Cherry Street
Macon, GA 31201
478-257-7255
ParishOnCherry.com

THE PERFECT PEAR
922 Carroll Street
Perry, GA 31069
478-224-7327

PHO SAIGON
3076 Riverside Drive
Macon, GA 31210
478-477-1117

PIETRO'S
1693 Bass Road
Macon, GA 31210
478-621-4328
PietroOrganics.com

RISTORANTE DA MARIA
875 James Currie Road
Dublin, GA 31021
478-275-8766
DublinFarm.com

THE ROOKERY
543 Cherry Street
Macon, GA 31201
478-746-8658
RookeryMacon.com

THE SWANSON
933 Carroll Street
Perry, GA 31069
478-987-1938
TheSwanson.com

TIC TOC ROOM
408 Martin Luther King Jr. Blvd
Macon, GA 31201
478-744-0123
HotPlatesGroup.com

Shrimp-salad BLT, Parish on Cherry

INDEX

Visit RebuildingMacon.org for additional recipies.

BEAU CABELL has been shooting photos since age twelve, when an aunt and uncle lent him an old Kodak camera. A native Midwesterner and graduate of the University of Missouri, he developed into a freelance photojournalist for the *Atlanta Journal-Constitution* and several wire services and later worked for the *Savannah Morning News* before joining *The Macon Telegraph* in 1984.

He has won many awards for his work, and during his years at *The Telegraph* has become particularly interested in food photography. What inspired him to produce the photos for this cookbook, he said, were the excellent chefs and restaurateurs he was able to work with. "They were outstanding people who were able to lend a sense of place and context about the food," Beau said, "In food, the tricks of the trade are usually closely-guarded secrets, but these people were really open and ready to share so much of their expertise."

While Beau works exclusively with today's sophisticated cameras and equipment, he still treasures that old Kodak camera, which his uncle later gave to him as a gift.

SKIPPY DAVIS is a freelance writer in Macon, retired after thirty years in journalism, during which she won more than twenty-five state and national writing awards. For almost twenty of her years in newspapers she worked as a reporter, editor and columnist with *The (Macon) Telegraph*. She also was Southeast regional reporter for *Women's Wear Daily* and a fashion writer for *The Florida-Times Union*.

In retirement, she enjoys gardening, making bead jewelry, working with animal rescue, and spending time with her three grown children and their families, which include seven absolutely adorable grandchildren.

REBUILDING MACON

OUR STORY

WE'RE STILL COOKING

REBUILDING MACON

IN PARTNERSHIP WITH THE COMMUNITY, Rebuilding Macon rehabilitates the homes of low-income homeowners—free of charge, particularly the elderly and disabled, so that they may live in warmth, safety and independence. We focus on the challenges elderly and disabled low-income homeowners face in their day to day lives. It has become the way of Rebuilding Macon to be readily equipped to face these challenges with full understanding so that practical solutions may be created for the low-income homeowners we serve.

Founded in 1992 as Christmas in April by Bruce Gerwig and a determined board of directors, 300 volunteers repaired 18 homes on Saturday, April 24. The organization worked the next year completing inspections, recruiting volunteer teams and matching them with projects for another one-day blitz in April. With each year came more and more calls for help, a reality that still holds true to this day. We recognized this and while the mission stayed the same, a shift in operations was needed. Then in 1999, thanks to a generous grant from the Peyton Anderson Foundation, Rebuilding Macon became a year-round organization that completes repairs throughout the year. Our Minor Home Repairs Program began and the number of people and households in Macon receiving services began to steadily increase.

Like any great recipe, Rebuilding Macon's programs have taken time to perfect. While operating year round, it became clear that some homeowner's situations posed immediate safety threats to their health and well-being. With this realization came the establishment of the Emergency Home Repairs Program and Good Samaritan Crew. Our Good Samaritan Crew is made up of mostly retired individuals from many different backgrounds and skill sets who get together every Tuesday, Wednesday, and Thursday and repair homes with critical safety issues. Every week they continually remind us that corny jokes are not overrated, chocolate for breakfast is not the worst thing you can do in life, and most importantly, that giving back to the community is essential to one's well-being.

In 2003, the Youth Enrichment Program was created to focus on cultivating and mentoring teens and young adults within our home repair program. Our objectives of the program include serving the unmet needs of the community, engaging young people in service projects that are challenging, rewarding and educational, promoting a greater understanding and appreciation for the diversity of their community, and instilling a lifetime ethic of service among young people. This program has proven to build bridges between youths and people of varied ages and backgrounds, including race, ethnicity, religious beliefs, gender and lifestyle. The program has grown from 270 teen volunteers repairing 30 homes in 2003, to more than 1,500 teens completing 120 repairs in 2016.

For more than two decades, churches, businesses, civic organizations, and the Macon/Bibb County government have been steadfast in their support of Rebuilding Macon. Volunteers continue to give their time, skills, and money to make a difference in the lives of all of us, because helping those in need improves the lives of everyone in Macon and Central Georgia. At the end of the day, our volunteers leave with skinned knees, sore backs, and most importantly, a great sense of accomplishment.

In 2009 Debra Rollins proposed the idea of publishing a cookbook as a way to increase awareness of our mission and maintain funding to the Board of Directors. Many thought she was a little out of her mind. For one, what did cooking have to do with rebuilding homes? However, Debra had a vision and those who doubted the idea quickly realized it was best to get behind her. She was determined to see that vision through. When 5,000 hard back copies landed on the front stoop of the Rebuilding Macon office, it was a sight that felt like a long time coming. The response to the cookbook was astonishing as the book seemed to sell faster than football tickets in the South, not to mention the amazing graphic design team was awarded a Gold Addy© Award for the book's design.

As many know, Debra Rollins has been with the organization since its inception in 1992, first as a volunteer and then as Executive Director in 1998. If you ask her about Macon, she'll say, "it's a work in progress." Debra has seen a vast amount of desperation through her years with Rebuilding Macon, but if there's one thing she knows, it's that a magnitude of community members continue to come together for the common cause of making Macon whole again, and local restaurant owners breathe fresh air into the city by upgrading commercial buildings and bringing in new business. So in Macon, cooking does have quite a bit in common with the work of a non-profit that rebuilds homes. It only seemed right to once again showcase this shared commitment in rebuilding Macon, and so now, six years later, we bring you *We're Still Cooking*.

All proceeds from the sale of this cookbook will support the programs of Rebuilding Macon. Funds raised will help build wheelchair ramps, replace roofs, paint homes and much, much more.

Give *We're Still Cooking* to your friends and family and help rebuild Macon. Many hearts will be touched—especially your own!